Pl

Power of the Air

CW01638002

266
Broadcasting:
Missions:
Chr ch

The Power of the Air

by

Peter and Pam Cousins

HODDER AND STOUGHTON
LONDON SYDNEY AUCKLAND TORONTO

FL79/ 13633 1079

266 COU

X1

Copyright © 1978 by Peter and Pam Cousins. First printed 1978. *ISBN 0 340 19652 1.* *All rights reserved. No part of this publication may be reproduced or transmitted in any form or by any means, electronic or mechanical, including photocopy, recording, or any information storage and retrieval system, without permission in writing from the publisher. This book is sold subject to the condition that it shall not, by way of trade or otherwise, be lent, re-sold, hired out or otherwise circulated without the publisher's prior consent in any form of binding or cover other than that in which this is published and without a similar condition including this condition being imposed on the subsequent purchaser.* *Printed in Great Britain for Hodder and Stoughton Limited, Mill Road, Dunton Green, Sevenoaks, Kent, by Cox & Wyman Ltd., London, Reading, and Fakenham*

Contents

1. The Radio Revolution 9
2. Christian Radio Rings the World 22
3. The Seychelles Story 30
4. Building on the Rock 48
5. Life on Mahé 56
6. Getting it Together 67
7. Looking for Trouble? 77
8. 'Respectable Aunty' 83
9. Is Anybody Listening? 107
10. Money Well Spent? 121
11. Business or Mission? 133
12. A New Kind of Missionary? 147
ENGLISH PROGRAMMES GUIDE 153
ABBREVIATIONS AND ADDRESSES 156

Foreword

This book has two objectives. In fact, some readers have suggested that it is really two books, not one. First, it is about the work of the Far East Broadcasting Association (FEBA), which operates the only British missionary radio station in the world, on Mahé in the Seychelles. Indeed, the book was originally undertaken at the invitation of the FEBA Council. Thus it will make a special appeal to FEBA supporters.

But it is impossible to understand the work of any missionary radio station without a certain amount of background knowledge. And missionary radio is a form of Christian outreach that has attracted a great deal of unthinking and uncritical interest. So we have also tried to provide a simple introduction to missionary radio — a subject which still awaits a full-scale definitive study. Although we have written a good deal about FEBA, the issues discussed and the problems outlined are relevant to *all* missionary radio outreach. So the book is not intended for FEBA supporters only, but for everybody who is interested in this rapidly developing and vital form of Christian ministry.

Although FEBA initiated the project and members of the Association have given help at every point, the views expressed are those of the authors. We take this opportunity of thanking those members of the Association who have given us help, members of the staff at Bangalore and Delhi, in the Seychelles and at Woking; friends in E. Africa and India who offered hospitality and information; Phil Booth of Radio Worldwide and other individuals and organisations involved in Christian radio work. A special word of thanks is due to Janice Taylor, formerly of Gipsy Hill College, who unwittingly provided the impulse for this book and to whom Chapter Two owes a great deal.

HAMMERSMITH PUBLIC LIBRARIES

CHAPTER I

The Radio Revolution

WHY EVER SHOULD a bishop burn Bibles? And what could such a bonfire possibly have to do with Christian radio in the 1970s? But he did — and it does.

The date was 1530. The Bibles (New Testaments to be exact) were burned at St Paul's Cross in the centre of London, England. The translator, William Tyndale, who had been forced to become a refugee in the Netherlands, was very happy about the whole operation. So (at the time) was Bishop Tunstal. He wanted to stamp out the circulation of the Bible in English, because it contradicted too much that he believed in. Tunstal reckoned he'd found a simple way to gain his objective when a merchant friend of Tyndale supplied a batch of the Testaments. (Tyndale got the money — so he could afford to take a long view of the affair.)

Tunstal bought the Testaments and burned them publicly. He knew it would take years to copy them again by hand. What he had apparently forgotten was that these Testaments were printed not copied. All Tyndale needed to do was to set the presses to work again.

People have laughed at Bishop Tunstal ever since. Yet he was no fool. He and Thomas More were entrusted by Henry VIII with important diplomatic business. Tunstal's failure wasn't due to lack of intelligence. He simply had not realised the significance of a new medium. Up till a century earlier, burning the Testaments would have made very good sense. Books were copied by hand, a process involving hours of work. A book was a rare and valuable object. Men would gather round to hear the owner read one aloud. Ordinary folk had little chance of owning even one book.

Then, about 1450, printing from movable type was discovered, an event that over the next five hundred years would change not only the history of mankind, but the way in which people thought — their whole approach to reality.

It's easy to laugh at Tunstal. Eighty years after the discovery of printing, he should have realised (we think) that a book could no longer be annihilated by simply burning single copies. But Tunstal was no more — and no less — of a fool than millions today who fail to realise that when Marconi transmitted the first radio signals in 1895 and made the first transatlantic broadcast in 1901 a new medium had appeared which would revolutionise communication just as radically as printing had done.

Today we are still adjusting to the new audio and video revolution. Radio, film, tape, television have changed and are still changing human thought patterns and life awareness. One aim of this book is to identify some of the opportunities and problems this revolution presents to Christians using radio to communicate their faith.

Viewed simply in terms of the number of radios in use, the size of the revolution is staggering. It owes a good deal to the cheapness of the transistor receiver. What cost £35 in 1965 was available for £5 by 1973. Whereas in 1922 the USA had 100,000 sets in use, the 1974 figure was 383 million. Between 1970 and 1974 the number of radios in Africa grew from 14 million to 22 million and in the Middle East from 13 million to 17 million. During this period of four years the total number of radios in Africa, Asia and Latin America increased by 25 per cent from 103 million to 129 million.

Of course these figures give no idea of the numbers using each set. Even in the west, several people are likely to listen together. Elsewhere, and especially in the Third World, many more will do so. People will club together to buy a radio. They will crowd into the home of the fellow villager who has bought his own. They will sit around in the evening when the day's work is over listening to whatever they can understand.

The impact is immeasurable. Formerly the only way in which an illiterate could make contact with any culture but his own was by listening to people who themselves had direct experience of other cultures. Even those who could read were limited to whatever books might be available. But today, as Alastair Cooke points out in his Guildhall Lectures for 1965,[1] 'This little thing (the transistor radio) held to the ear brings into the life of a boy in the jungle or a tribesman in the desert, news of the towns and the continents, of the politics and uprisings . . . as a link with the real world, the radio set is far more powerful than the printing press was to the scholars and the church. As a weapon of propaganda whether true or false, it is mightier than all the pens and most of the swords . . .'

One's first experience of a short wave set is awe-inspiring. As the pointer moves across the dial, so the voices come from all over the world. London, Washington, Moscow, Peking, the Vatican — and a multitude of smaller stations: Cuba, Sweden, Poland. Radio Moscow's many large stations provide 332 hours' broadcasting in 78 languages. Every day. The amount of money spent on these external radio services shows how convinced governments are of the importance and effectiveness of radio.

Totalitarian governments have also made powerful use of radio to inform and indoctrinate their own peoples. This is not merely because radio, which depends on the spoken not the written word, can be understood by old and young, educated and illiterate, nor even — though this is important — because loudspeakers can reach people everywhere, in cafés, public buildings, town and village open spaces as well as homes. To a far greater degree than print, radio can have an almost hypnotic effect. As one respondent to a survey put it: 'I live right inside

1. *The Camel Driver and the Transistor*.

radio when I listen. I lose myself more easily in radio than in a book.'[2] J. T. Klapper claims that the broadcasting media can 'provide their audiences with a sense of participation, personal access and reality which approximate face to face contact.'[3] Sporting events, international crises, natural disasters are brought into people's homes as they happen. During the war and at other times of stress, this potential of radio has been exploited powerfully by men as diverse as Adolf Hitler, Franklin Roosevelt, Winston Churchill. As broadcasts Churchill's war-time speeches did infinitely more to boost the morale of the nation than they could ever have done in cold print. The point, of course, is that they were given 'warm' not 'cold'. Hearers respond to all sorts of 'signals' in the spoken word that they would overlook in reading, even if it were possible (which it isn't) to express them in print. A whole nation can be made to feel as one through radio in a way that makes print seem powerless.

We can see how completely this was overlooked fifty years ago by the fact that the new medium was called 'wireless'. As McLuhan points out[4] this is very much like calling a car a horseless carriage. It suggests that radio is another variety of telegraph system different in not using a cable link, important because of its use for conveying information. The emotional and cultural significance of the medium was ignored.

From one angle then we can see radio as uniting vast communities. As people listen to the same news bulletins, weather forecasts, comedy shows, the nation is at one. Yet from another viewpoint radio appeals strongly to small minorities, and is a means by which like-minded individuals and small groups can breathe the same air and affirm common values and interests. Illustrations of this are endless. We may mention programmes in minority languages, such as Gaelic or Welsh; local radio stations; all-night programmes with their offer of intimacy

2. *Understanding Media*, M. McLuhan (Penguin edition), p. 318.
3. *Effects of Mass Communication* (Free Press of Glencoe, 1960), p.111
4. Op. cit., p. 324.

without commitment; programmes for anglers, housewives, pensioners. Above all, perhaps, the teenage network which expresses a sort of international tribalism within western culture as a whole.

The relevance of this last factor to Christian radio is obvious. Radio Vatican keeps Roman Catholics the world over in touch with Rome. As we shall see, thousands of radio programmes remind Christians who are either isolated or in a minority that they belong to a fellowship that spans the world. Letters written in response to programmes transmitted from the Seychelles and other similar agencies underline the importance of this.

'I have been listening to your programme regularly and have received spiritual benefit from it. Believe me, your programmes are very profitable and pleasant. We who live hundreds of miles away from any church and where only one or two Christians live nor do we have any Pastor, we listen to your radio programmes which give us the feeling of being in a church listening to godly messages. We thank you very much for this.'

'Bastar is a backward area and is overshadowed with darkness, but our refuge is the Lord and his word and a transistor which brings in the messages you broadcast through which we receive fresh food every day. Thanks be to the Lord for this.'

Since radio is such an important and effective medium it's not surprising that Christians should make use of it. The discovery of printing in the west revolutionised Christian communication. The Bible was translated into the languages of the common people and widely distributed. Religious books were owned and studied by people who would otherwise have depended on whatever the local priest might say from the pulpit. The Reformation resulted, in part, from the discovery of printing. Is it possible that radio might be equally important?

Certainly there are today immense obstacles hindering Christian witness. The command to 'go to people everywhere' becomes more difficult to obey as the years pass. 'It took a million years,' John Taylor affirms[5] 'to produce *the first* billion human beings. It took only a hundred years to produce the second billion, by the 1850s. It took only fifteen years to produce the fourth billion by 1973. And the next forty years will add to the world's population more people than the whole history of mankind has done to date.' At the same time, the number of missionaries and full-time Christian workers is declining in most denominations. It has been estimated that each full-time Christian worker needs to evangelise seven new people every day simply to keep pace with the birthrate — to say nothing of the forty million which represents his or her 'share' of the existing population. In any case, while only 10 per cent of the world's population speak English, 90 per cent of full-time Christian workers function among this 10 per cent leaving the other 90 per cent of mankind to the remaining 10 per cent of workers. Although there is an impressive tradition of mass evangelism stretching back via Billy Graham, D. L. Moody, Whitfield and John Wesley to St Peter himself, it can hardly stand this strain. Of course the New Testament nowhere suggests that evangelism should be the responsibility of 'full-time' workers and happily Christians everywhere are coming to see that this is the privilege of all God's people. But although the church is growing, and growing very fast in some parts of the world, this growth does not begin to match the world population explosion.

Yet this is not the only problem. In many places Christians are not free to tell others about Jesus. We talk glibly of living in a 'global village' and speak as if modern methods of transport had broken down the frontiers separating nations. But the fact is that over a billion people live behind the Iron or the Bamboo Curtain through which missionaries and in some cases even Bibles may not pass. In the quarter of the world's surface controlled by Communism even a nation's own citizens are likely to be hindered from public witness. At the same time,

5. *Enough is Enough*, J. Taylor (SCM, London, 1975), p. 14. (The 'billion' is an American one, i.e. one thousand million.)

the whole population is exposed to anti-Christian teaching and propaganda through all the communications media, at work and in school.

Communist nations may be the best known, but they are certainly not the only ones to forbid or restrict Christian witness. Most Muslim states, containing over 150 million people, are associated with this sort of opposition or downright persecution. So are numerous other countries under despotic rule.

Faced by these two difficulties, many Christians have come to think that radio is part of God's answer to the church's problems. So far as the population explosion is concerned, radio offers the chance of reaching not just thousands, but millions of listeners. We may cite a conversation with a missionary doctor from India. Although run off his feet with hospital work, he makes time to tape programmes in Telugu which are then broadcast back from the FEBA Seychelles station into the area where he works, and even into the hospital wards. Asked if he really considered the expense in time and money was justified, he answered simply: 'I can see no other way of meeting the population explosion.'

Perhaps it is significant that he works in India. Everybody who visits the subcontinent remembers the overwhelming impact of the sheer numbers of people who crowd the cities. It's like a constant London rush-hour. Humanly speaking there is no chance that the small Indian church (no more than 2½ per cent, very patchily distributed geographically and socially) can tell these millions about Jesus. Radio can make all the difference here, directed to the 14 million receivers in use in India.

If this is the case in India, how much more important radio can be in China. Here the presence of a vast population and a tiny Christian minority is only half the problem. In China, public witness is out of the question. Private worship is dangerous enough! But radio waves, first used for intercontinental communication in 1901, are well able to penetrate the Iron and

Bamboo Curtains which fifty years later cut off the people of Eastern Europe, Russia and China from contact with Christians outside the Communist block.

Some of the listeners are completely ignorant of Christianity; some are hostile. 'Right at the start,' writes a Russian listener, 'I want to explain that I do not believe in God and on the whole I am an atheist by persuasion. Nevertheless your programmes have interested me, even though not as one who believes in what you say. I have become interested in the history of the Christian religion, but it is very difficult to obtain the necessary literature which would supply the information in which I am interested. Therefore I shall be very grateful to you if you would send me the book you are offering, *Daily Readings for a Christian*, or any other religious book.'

Another is sufficiently aroused to protest; 'Whoever asked you to grind such rubbish to us? Or has God offended you in not giving you a mind? Here in our country children from the age of three know there is no God.'

One Government response has been to 'jam' the broadcasts. But it seems unlikely that the deafening roar and high-pitched scream of the special transmitters used for this purpose will ever be totally effective. For one thing, jamming is only about 50 per cent effective; listeners still hear, though with difficulty. It is also so expensive that mere cost means it cannot be used as much as Communist leaders might wish. In fact, the USSR has now given up jamming religious broadcasts, although its jamming of political programmes inevitably affects other transmissions.

It's hard to exaggerate the reassurance and encouragement Christian radio can offer oppressed and isolated Christians behind closed frontiers. Here is one such listener: 'With unquenching thirst we wait for your broadcasts which bring us comfort and conviction. My husband, eleven-year-old girl and I live in the mountains sixty kilometres from a church — we can go there only once a month.' There is even an audience for special programmes in which the Bible is read at dictation speed so that Chinese and Russian believers can do something themselves to combat the chronic shortage of Bibles in those countries. For them, in this context at least, printing might never have been discovered!

Today we can see the strategic importance of Christian radio, if we will only open our eyes. The twin problems of the population explosion and closed frontiers are plain. But when Christian radio began — almost by accident — nobody seems to have realised the significance of the new medium.

Late in 1920 in Pittsburgh, Pennsylvania, the staff of a new local station, KDKA, were facing the problem of deciding what sort of programmes to put out on Sunday. One of them, a member of the Calvary Church Choir, suggested that perhaps his church might agree to broadcast its service. We can gauge how far the importance of the occasion was realised when we note that the first radio sermon was preached not by the rector, but by his associate. Although the rector was present and the associate invited him to preach, the suggestion was declined.

It was not long before Christians came to see the immense potential of radio and throughout the twenties evangelistic and devotional programmes proliferated all over North America. Here it was possible for anybody to buy broadcasting time since the stations were privately owned commercial enterprises. The situation was very different in Britain, where the BBC was the only source of programmes. It had an important and lively religious broadcasting department, developed between 1922 and 1939 which ensured that the United Kingdom never experienced the mixed blessing of sponsored religious radio.

Quite naturally, both the BBC and the North American stations continued the tradition established by KDKA in Pittsburgh. Not that there was any question of conscious imitation — it was inevitable that the first religious programmes should amount to no more than putting on the air the activities normally carried on in and by churches. Sometimes these might be broadcast from the studio, sometimes they were outside (or in the USA 'remote') broadcasts. In any case they took the form of church services, community hymn singing, concerts of religious music, devotional talks, and also (in North America) evangelistic meetings and Bible exposition.

The importance of this assumption cannot be overstated. It was simply taken for granted that Christian radio should provide the sort of material that the churches were already offering to their members and interested unbelievers. Even today most supporters of Christian radio make the same assumption — and so do a terrifying proportion of the people actively engaged in this form of Christian service.

This tendency was inevitable. Every new medium needs time for new artistic forms to be invented or adapted. When radio began it was generally regarded simply as a means of making more widely available the secular activities that listeners valued, but soon this objective led to the introduction of new forms and techniques. A news bulletin, for example, is apparently a straightforward substitute for a newspaper. But nobody can read through the *Daily Telegraph* or the *New York Herald Tribune* in the time available for a newscast; the kind of sentence structure suitable for reading in a newspaper is not the best for listening to; consequently, as everybody knows, a news bulletin is quite different from a newspaper.

Thus over the years radio has developed a wide range of new and distinctive types of programme. Listeners are so familiar with them that they take them for granted; five-minute talks, interviews, panel discussions, documentaries, listener participation programmes including 'phone-ins', spot announcements, record request programmes, magazine programmes. Unfortunately, the people responsible for Christian radio outreach and Christians who support Christian radio have generally been slow to move away from traditional 'religious' forms, and too often even today Christian radio is in this respect forty years behind the times.

It is easy to see the advantages of using radio to preach the gospel and teach the Bible. But how can Christians get on the air? No radio station is going to offer them the use of its equipment without good reason.

In countries with a single state-administered broadcasting network Christians can work within it. They may influence it from inside, by becoming producers, especially in the religious broadcasting department, or they may work from outside by offering programmes which will appeal to the authorities as being likely to attract listeners. This is the position in India, for example, and still to a great extent in Britain.

Since 1973 there have been commercial radio stations in Britain, but this has made little difference so far as Christian broadcasting is concerned. True, the stations are financed by advertising, but political and religious advertising is prohibited. Nobody can buy programme time, and the only new factor involved is that since these stations (like the new BBC ones) are local, they give Christians in the neighbourhood a further opportunity to offer programmes for presentation, or to feature in news and magazine programmes.

The situation is completely different in the USA and other countries where anybody is allowed (subject to certain conditions) to set up a station and to finance it by payments from both commercials and sponsored programmes. In the USA, stations are run by universities and churches. 'Gospel' radio stations, providing a staple diet of religious programmes, have become big business.

During the twenties and thirties Christian radio programmes multiplied all over the USA. Although it can be argued that the sponsorship system tended to encourage lower cultural standards, and in spite of the many shortcomings of the small commercial stations, here was a unique opportunity for evangelism and Bible teaching.

It is important to be clear that two possible courses of action were available. One was to buy time on an existing station. Most people in Britain are familiar with this concept, thanks to Radio Luxembourg, which for some time included in its schedule of pop music a number of Christian programmes.

Later the 'pirate' stations such as Radio Caroline offered the same opportunity. Many British believers rejoiced because 'the gospel' was being preached far more frequently by this means than could ever have been permitted by the BBC. They were sometimes disturbed to hear on the same wavelength programmes put out by semi-Christian sects such as Herbert W. Armstrong's Radio Church of God, but willing to accept this competition as the price of freedom to preach Christ.

Unfortunately Radio Luxembourg discovered in the end that Christian programmes were so unattractive that no advertiser wanted his commercials to appear anywhere near them. As Radio Luxembourg is in business to make money, it decided to discontinue English language religious programmes. (At the time of writing, it has allowed one such broadcast in the short-wave band.)

A number of such programmes are still broadcast by commercial stations in Europe, but they tend to be restricted to the least popular listening times (late night and very early morning), and they are vulnerable to being axed for commercial reasons.

Recently Radio Ceylon (now Radio Sri Lanka), the Luxembourg of the Indian subcontinent, has changed its policy in the reverse direction. In the mid-1960s, due to the unwise cultural content of the religious programmes supplied to them, all such programmes were discontinued. However, it decided in 1971, for good financial reasons, to offer its facilities once again to religious groups. (The programmes were not, however, beamed into Ceylon itself, which is strongly Buddhist.) This has provided a most valuable opportunity for Christians and Christian groups, since Radio Sri Lanka has a strong popular appeal. Subsequently, a long-term agreement incorporating several severe restrictions has been concluded with a Christian radio organisation (see p. 136). But the episode illustrates the uncertainty of working through commercial agencies.

This uncertainty can to some extent be avoided by adopting

a second course of action. Christian agencies can provide their own stations. This was not at all uncommon in the USA during the twenties and thirties. So it was not surprising that missionary-minded Americans utilised it in other countries.

CHAPTER 2

Christian Radio Rings the World

TODAY THERE ARE over 50 missionary radio stations scattered about the world. In 1931 there were none. This chapterglances at the story of four missionary radio ogranisations, each of which *began* as a single station but which now between them operate some 48 transmitters.

The first missionary radio station in the world was HCJB, 'The Voice of the Andes', at Quito, Ecuador. It is significant that Clarence Jones, one of its founders, had been associated with gospel radio in the USA since 1922 — as a member of a brass quartet that accompanied radio evangelist Paul Rader. In 1928 his concern for evangclism led him to seek a site in South America where a radio station might be set up, but it was not until 1929 that he met Reuben Larson, a young missionary working in Ecuador, and teamed up with him. On August 15, 1930, Larson secured a licence to establish the first radio station in Ecuador. 'This wireless installation,' the licence stipulated, 'shall be used by the contractors for the reception and transmission of matters of a scientific, literary, artistic and religious nature.' (Sixteen years later, the cultural and social value of HCJB's work was recognised when the station received one of Ecuador's highest honours, the Decoration of the National Order of Merit in the degree of Knight.)

Like every radio station, the one at Quito must have an international call sign, but seeing it was the first in Ecuador there was complete freedom to select any combination of four letters, provided the first two were HC, the code allotted to

Ecuador. Prayerful and astute, the missionaries chose Heralding Christ Jesus' Blessings, or in Spanish, *Hoy Cristo Jesu Bendice* ('today Christ Jesus blesses').

On Christmas Day, 1931, they went on the air, using a 250-watt transmitter and operating from a half-finished sheep shed. They broadcast for half an hour on that occasion, but soon extended to two hours a day, in one language. There were at the time only six receivers in Quito — and that was as far as the signal could be heard!

Today HCJB is on the air 24 hours of every day, often in three languages simultaneously, with up to three frequencies in each language and using a total of 460,000 watts of power. A new 500 kilowatt transmitter is being built. Since 1949 HCJB has been associated with the work of Radio HOXO, a local station situated in Panama, which broadcasts throughout the day, combining evangelistic programmes with news, good music and cultural features. In 1972, FM stereo programmes began from HCJB Guyaquil, in Ecuador's largest city, broadcasting mainly music and news with Spanish evangelistic programmes interspersed. Also in Guyaquil, the All Ecuador Gospel Network provides both cultural features and taped gospel programmes free of charge to commercial stations throughout Ecuador. There are plans to broadcast from Hawaii. In 1961 HCJB-TV went on the air, enabling people to see, as well as hear, the good news.

By 1946, medical help was needed to care for a staff team of 75 members. It seemed quite natural to combine with this a clinic for the local Indian population and 1955 saw the opening of the Rimmer Memorial Hospital in Quito. Three years later, another hospital was inaugurated 150 miles away at Shell Mera on the fringes of Ecuador's eastern jungle. Both were paid for largely through the contributions of American listeners to 'Back to the Bible' and 'Morning Cheer' religious programmes.

Among the other activities of HCJB we may mention the Bible Institute of the Air which since 1947 has taught the

Bible to local pastors and Christian workers through correspondence courses and radio lessons; the Evangelism Department which functions all over Ecuador; the printing department; and a hydro-electric plant which provides power for the seven transmitters and the other needs of the mission. No wonder the World Radio Missionary Fellowship has 197 staff members plus 255 employees and an annual budget of three million dollars (1975 figure).

The West Africa Broadcasting Association deserves a place in any list of dotty Christian societies and clubs. It was founded (and 'officially incorporated in the State of Illinois') by three young students at Wheaton College. Abe Thiessen, Bill Watkins and Merle Steeley had chosen an impressive title for their organisation, but there was not much more to it than that. 'Prayer,' they would have said, and 'a sense of the Lord's leading,' these were their sole assets; they possessed no resources, no mailing list of interested friends, and above all no contacts in Africa who could advise them where to locate a station.

One night a visitor turned up at the WABA meeting. Norma Bloomquist, a former Lutheran missionary, assured them they would be welcome in Liberia where she had worked as Director of Literacy. Invited by the President to visit him and talk the scheme over, they sank every available cent in an air ticket for Bill Watkins and waited for news of a break-through. Disappointingly, Watkins was told to re-apply a year later. Instead he stayed in Monrovia and began a dreary round of visits to government officials, all of whom, quite naturally, had more important things to talk about than the plans of the WABA. Finally he invaded the Postmaster General's breakfast room and explained his scheme to the dressing-gowned official. It was not long before the necessary permit arrived.

There was still no money. By September 1951 the WABA assets totalled 2,500 dollars, hardly enough for one passage to Liberia. It was not surprising that a well-meaning Christian friend advised them to forget this new-fangled idea and get preaching like men! But the support they needed seemed to be assured when the Sudan Interior Mission took them under its wing and helped them to secure a sea-shore location near Monrovia. The call sign allocated was appropriate — it was not difficult to interpret ELWA as Eternal Love Winning Africa.

Their troubles were by no means at an end. Construction work was not easy in a country where 200 inches of rain falls in six months every year, washing away roads and destroying bridges. 'Mud, sweat and tears!' was how one missionary described it. There was the occasion when a newly-arrived expert pointed out that the painstakingly constructed studio and generator building had been wrongly sited, leaving no room for either expansion or an aerial array — and the whole job had to be done again, while support from the USA dwindled as progress appeared to have ceased.

Yet on January 18, 1954, ELWA went on the air, broadcasting three hours per day, while the bustle and noise of the building operation continued unchecked except when a station break or announcement made silence necessary. Today, five transmitters beam signals not only to Liberia and West Africa but in a wider arc across Africa from the Congo to Equatorial Africa, the Middle East and North Africa. Five frequencies are used to transmit programmes in 15 tribal languages as well as English, French and Arabic. (Supplementing and overlapping their work have been signals from Radio Voice of the Gospel in Addis Ababa, from the Swaziland station of Trans World Radio and from FEBA Seychelles.)

Like HCJB, ELWA has moved from supplying the medical needs of its own ELWA Radio Village to serving the local community. Since 1965, a 39-bed modern hospital has extended its usefulness to the point where it averages 145 admissions a month and cares for more than 3,000 persons per month in the out-patient clinic. The ELWA Academy and the ELWA Village School meet the educational needs of the families of a staff which comprises 200 Liberian workers and some 60 missionaries.

Just one month after ELWA began broadcasting, the 'Voice of Tangier' was heard for the first time—a 2½-kilowatt transmitter providing programmes in European languages: Serbo-Croatian, Roumanian, German, Spanish and English. Paul Freed, formerly a Youth for Christ worker, had felt a concern for missionary radio to evangelise Spain, and had made an arrangement with an American who already had a station and permit in Tangier. He agreed to build the transmitter and antennae and to lease the facilities to Freed. By 1959, Trans World Radio was broadcasting in more than twenty languages.

During the late 1950s Freed visited Monte Carlo to investigate the possibility of making a rather similar agreement with the authorities there. They possessed a massive transmitter building, built by the Germans during World War Two, but it contained no equipment. Surely there were possibilities here? The matter became urgent when the Moroccan government announced in April 1959 that all radio in the country was to be nationalised by the end of the year. Faced with the end of his Tangier work, Freed returned to Monte Carlo, and negotiated an unusual contract. TWR would pay 500,000 dollars to Monte Carlo in six instalments during the year; this would provide for the installation of equipment which would be the property of Radio Monte Carlo, but TWR would be repaid by a ten-year lease, with an indefinite number of renewals.

TWR went on the air from Monte Carlo on October 16, 1960. In April 1966 they received permission to use Monte Carlo's 400-kilowatt medium-wave transmitter after 10 p.m. This greatly increased audiences in Europe, where short-wave listening is a minority interest. As a result of this development TWR has become synonymous with Christian radio for many in the UK since it is responsible for the medium-wave broadcasts that most listeners can actually hear.

By 1962, Freed was looking for a second transmitter site, this time in the Caribbean. Plans were made to build in Curacao but proximity to a large international airport presented problems and so — a fortnight before construction was scheduled to start — the whole project was transferred to the adjacent island of Bonaire, where sea and salt-flats offered conditions ideal for transmitting short waves. Today Bonaire uses shortwave transmitters of 50 kilowatts and 250 kilowatts, together with the largest medium-wave transmitter (500 kilowatts) in the western hemisphere, to broadcast round the clock in 15 languages.

The dynamism and thrust of TWR have been remarkable. Freed quotes with approval the remark of a Voice of America director (Voice of America is broadly comparable with the BBC World Service): 'The only recourse open to the VOA is to have more power than competitors on the same frequency and to be more flexible in the use of frequencies. This is jungle warfare. Victory goes to the strong, the smart and the quick.' TWR has showed all of these qualities as it has established transmitters on Bonaire in 1964, Cyprus (1974), in Swaziland (1974), Guam (1975) and Sri Lanka, formerly known as Ceylon (1976). Total power is 50,000 kilowatts and there are some 350 staff workers administering an annual budget of approximately £4 million. Whereas other Christian radio societies focus on one area, TWR feels called to set up its own transmitters in every part of the globe.

The Far East Broadcasting Company was founded in 1941 by three young men whose total resources amounted to $1,000. Two of them were already not unknown: Robert Bowman was the 'second mate' on the 'Good Ship Grace', a programme heard daily in the Los Angeles area and nationally, once a week. William J. Roberts was pastor of a large church in the Los Angeles area and was on the air daily in 'The Family Bible Hour'. It was the third member of the group, Robert Broger, who had just been discharged from the Navy and who shared their concern for radio evangelism in the Far East, who sailed in 1946 to arrange station facilities.

After drawing a blank in Shanghai, he went on to Manila in the Philippines. Here an official who studied the application for a radio franchise posed an apparently unanswerable question: 'You have not stated how you will be financed nor the amount of power you will be using.' Although puzzled, he accepted Broger's answer: 'We believe God will supply all the money through dedicated Christians . . . God will supply our needs.'

It proved extremely difficult to find a suitable site near enough to Manila, but two Christian businessmen were able to offer a plot that suited the requirements of both FEBC and the government. Broger used his last $50 to secure the option. The Philippine Radio Commission accepted the property as suitable but the franchise was good only if FEBC were on the air by April 14, 1948, less than eighteen months after purchase of the site. The question of the power to be used had been settled by an unknown official who had pencilled out the suggested 'ten thousand watts' and substituted 'unlimited power'.

In the event it proved necessary to seek an extension of the deadline. But even the revised date, June 4, seemed out of the question when three days earlier one of the circuits failed. Efforts to obtain a further extension were unsuccessful, and just before 6 p.m. on the 4th Broger got back to Radio City after a final fruitless attempt. There was no alternative — they would have to go on the air without testing the transmitter. An overloaded circuit blew and station DZAS went off the air — but they had succeeded in broadcasting for two hours and the franchise was secure.

FEBC began with a one-kilowatt transmitter. By 1976 the output from 24 international stations in five countries totalled more than 1,000 kilowatts providing 242 programme hours per day. From 1948 to 1956, development was concentrated in Manila but 1957–58 saw the establishment of two stations on Okinawa and in 1960 another large station (originally 50 kilowatts but now increased to 250 kilowatts) was set up in San

Francisco to reach the whole of South America. Today the staff of FEBC Radio International exceeds 500 people; approximately three-quarters of them are nationals of the 'target' nations. Among their responsibilities is dealing with an average of 31,000 letters per month (June 1975 – February 1976) from the listening audience.

While the aim of FEBC is 'to communicate Jesus Christ around the world', this is accomplished through a wide variety of programmes. In 1966 their station DZFE, 'Manila's Fine Music Station', was awarded the First Annual Citizens' Award of Merit Presentation from the Citizens' Council for Mass Media, the national radio and television organisation of the Philippines.

It is no coincidence that every Christian radio organisation listed in this chapter is North American. As we have already seen, there are historical reasons why the concept of radio evangelism and Bible teaching developed in the USA. But within the FEBC 'family' there is one autonomous British unit, the only British Christian radio station in the world and the immediate occasion of this book.

CHAPTER 3

The Seychelles Story

FOR AIRCRAFT ENTHUSIASTS in Europe, the Farnborough air show is probably the most important event of the year. Visitors from all over the world come to this small Hampshire town to see (and hear) the latest developments in design and production.

But the little group of Christian young men from Cheam, 20 miles away, had another reason for going to Farnborough. The North Downs Gospel Fellowship were using stereo recording equipment — unusual in those days — to make yet another tape to send to Manila for use by FEBC.

Among the members of the NDGF was a young businessman called Douglas Malton, with a concern for Christian radio and in particular for the work of FEBC. He often tells the story of the two old ladies standing side by side on 'Decimal Day', February 1971. As they looked at the new coinage which was now to become legal tender, one turned anxiously to the other.

'Ethel,' she said, 'I don't think I'll ever understand this new money.'

'Don't you worry, my dear,' returned her friend. 'Myself, I don't think it'll ever catch on.'

This, says Douglas Malton, was just how British Christians felt about Christian radio in the 1950s. Long accustomed to the dignified tones of the BBC, they had heard of commercial radio and feared that if it came to Britain it would be in effect a landing strip for the devil. They knew next to nothing of its use for Christian communication — and they cared even less. The North Downs Gospel Fellowship was a remarkable exception to the general rule.

Also from Cheam was John Wheatley. An engineer working in various parts of the world for Cable and Wireless, he knew more than most people about radio and felt frustrated by Christians' apathy and ignorance. Later he resigned from Cable and Wireless in order to seek an opening in Christian radio, eventually applying to FEBC.

But before this happened a business trip to Kuwait had led him to take an equally important decision. For it was there he found a wife. Alice's American missionary society had sent her there to learn Arabic and teach in a mission school. This was a second best. She had originally felt 'called' to China, but the Communist takeover there slammed the door in the face of Christian missions. This was why John found her in the only place where the work of Cable and Wireless overlapped that of her missionary society.

After the wedding John and Alice spent a short time in England, then went to Alice's home. In the USA they must not only have the FEBC appointment confirmed, but also (in accordance with FEBC policy [see p. 125] raise the cost of their passage to the Philippines and their first year's living expenses, with promises of regular support.

For a start they were living and working in the eastern United States, far from FEBC's base in California. They soon found that in 1953 most congregations and clergy in the east, although well aware of the possibilities of local radio, seemed as unaware of the ministry of FEBC as their UK brothers and sisters.

In the end they made themselves mobile, driving around with a caravan, telephoning ministers and getting introductions wherever they went. But they made contact with any number of churches, shared their concern for Christian radio, and finally secured the money they needed. Then they were off to Manila, John as a transmitter engineer and Alice to work in the record library where she eventually became responsible for all traffic of tapes and recordings.

Douglas Malton was at the farewell meeting for the Wheatleys when they left for the USA. He was still uncertain how best to alert Christians in the UK to the *facts* of Christian radio, (which, as we have seen had been flourishing for years in some parts of the world), and to its immense missionary potential.

When John and Alice visited the UK during their first furlough in 1959, the two men shared their concern. They agreed to try and set up a support group in the UK for FEBC. John and Alice were in the country for only four months, so Douglas would have to take responsibility. The first step was to arrange a meeting of people who would be interested. They gathered in the home of Seymour and Elsie Alexander, a couple who, like other members of that initial group, were to maintain a close and practical interest in FEBA in succeeding years.

At one point in the discussions of this group, Douglas suggested it might be wise for someone to take notes — and found himself promptly established as the first honorary secretary (later to become Chairman) of the Far Eastern Broadcasting Associates of Great Britain, the forerunner of similar groups in India, Australia and New Zealand. Their aims were simple — to make known in Britain what God was doing through missionary radio. Wherever groups of Christians requested a visit, they would show American films about FEBC or John's own film-strip, 'A Visit to Christian Radio City Manila'. Douglas, Hein Velissarides and one or two others bore the burden of this deputation work.

Closely involved too was Douglas's new wife, Joan. As a senior radiographer at the Mildmay Hospital she was used to putting missionaries at their ease and soon became accustomed to looking after visitors, doing a certain amount of clerical work as the situation demanded. The first office of this embryonic organisation was the kitchen of their small flat.

(Joan's parents, Stanley and Nellie Mansell, were later to play an important part in the FEBC/FEBA work. For four years after retiring from the Civil Service Stanley overhauled and serviced the diesel generators for the FEBC transmitter on Okinawa, broadcasting to China: he was secretary in the Woking office for a while and in 1971 served as Field Director on Mahé while the Wheatleys took a furlough.)

The first full-time secretarial help came from Philip Jones, pastor of Woking Baptist Church, which still produces a weekly programme, 'Wondrous Story'. He continued to serve in this way until after the move to the permanent Surrey address that has become well known to supporters everywhere. It was in 1966 while Douglas and Joan were househunting that they realised the grounds of the house they were currently interested in would provide room to build both living quarters for the secretary and offices for the Associates. Now, in 1977, that accommodation at 'Sky Waves' in St Paul's Road, Woking (a few hundred yards from the first mosque ever built in Britain!), houses a staff of about nine handling post to and from all parts of the world, and has become inadequate.

From the outset, Bob Bowman, the founder and president of FEBC (see pp. 27–29), showed interest in this British support group, coming to England at least once a year for a programme of visits and consultations planned by the Associates. On a trip in 1963, he brought a request from America. It was intended to establish at Bangalore, India, a new headquarters to co-ordinate the FEBC programming of the subcontinent, hitherto centred in Delhi. In view of the links between Britain and India, and given the existence of some anti-American sentiment, could the Associates supply an engineer to work in the studio?

Construction of the Bangalore centre was financed by students of the Moody Bible Institute, Chicago, who adopted it as their missionary 'project' for 1962. Especially active in this had been Ben Das, himself a student, from India. By 1964 the time had come to equip the studio.

Enter another Christian radio enthusiast, Wyndham Mathieson, a chiropractor living in rural Devon. A visit from John

Wheatley, a film of the Philippines work, and a realisation of the need for tapes, led him to decide to establish a studio in his own house, where programmes could be recorded. The equipment chosen was the best available. A room was set aside and suitably furnished. He was no technician and there were frustrations in plenty. The cable ordered, for example, proved to be thicker and stronger than was really necessary. But the studio was used and tapes were sent from Exeter to Manila.

Then came a most unexpected and disturbing challenge. Wyndham sat late into the night preparing for a meeting the next day at which he was going to share the vision of radio work. He had already looked through the current news booklet, the FEBA *Broadcaster*, but now he noticed a 'P.T.O.' in the corner of one page. He found himself confronted by a list — items of equipment needed for the Bangalore studio. With an overwhelming shock he realised that everything needed was there in his own house.

No man who has set his heart on achieving something finds it easy to realise that God appears to have some other purpose. Could he let it all go? With a not unnatural struggle he made his decision. If someone would come and fetch the equipment, it should go to India.

By this time, a studio engineer for Bangalore had been appointed. Malcolm Fidge's career with EMI was interrupted by National Service; once this was over he began to look elsewhere to gain more studio experience so that he might be better equipped for Christian radio work. Against all the odds he obtained a job with Radio Free Europe.

As Malcolm and Maureen Fidge faced the first ever candidates' board of the Associates, they had no idea of the concern felt about this appointment . . . It seemed right to take the step, but at that time every penny the Associates received was earmarked for the work of FEBC. Would that support suffer if money was diverted to the Fidges? In the event a decisive increase in gifts enabled the Associates to fulfil their financial obligations.

Arriving at the Mathieson home to check the equipment, Malcolm found it identical with what he had already been used to at EMI. As for the thick cable, however unsuitable for a domestic studio, it was just the thing for Bangalore. And it turned out to be the right length too!

Meanwhile John Wheatley found himself travelling once more, now as overseas programme director for FEBC, though he retained technical responsibility for frequency management. The job entailed visiting programme suppliers and advising on technical problems.

An extensive tour of India in 1962, where he surveyed reception conditions, led to serious consideration being given to the need for a new transmitting base which would enable programmes to reach the subcontinent more effectively. FEBC was effective only in the southern half of India. A glance at the map will show why. From Manila the radio waves have an ideal journey for 2,000 out of 3,000 miles to southern India and Ceylon. As they 'bounce' between the earth's surface and the ionosphere, the sea provides an excellent trampoline! Whereas the reflection points between Manila and north India or Pakistan are the rugged mountainous masses of north Burma and Tibet which weaken the signal, so that broadcasts were not heard clearly, if at all. Yet more than half the total population of India's 600 millions live in the northern regions and there are proportionately more radio sets there as well. Additionally there are the people of Pakistan estimated to total 110 millions.

But where could FEBC establish a new base? Had the islands of the Indian ocean anything to offer? The Cocos Islands seemed at first the most suitable since the existing air service would make access easy. An application was sent by FEBC to the Australian government which administered the islands, but the response was cool. The Seychelles were mentioned at this stage but quickly dismissed as being far too isolated without an airport.

The years slipped by until in 1967 fresh moves were made

to secure a location. The Maldives were considered, but rejected. Then came news that the British government intended to construct an airport on Mahé, the largest of the Seychelles islands. That same year the news was also received that the air service to the Cocos Islands was being withdrawn.

In Manila John Wheatley attended an important meeting of FEBC directors which considered the need and unanimously settled for a new transmitter base. So important was the decision that it was voted on by secret ballot, a most unusual procedure. However FEBC was by now vastly over-extended and it was agreed that new sources of revenue, staff and equipment must be found. For the first time the suggestion was made that the Associates in the United Kingdom might be willing to back up the project. The Seychelles, the most likely site, was after all a British Crown Colony. An official approach must be made to the Foreign and Commonwealth Office in London where John was due in April 1967 for the International Christian Broadcasters' Conference. The Associates' committee received the FEBC request. Checking the state of their bank account (£400), they got on their knees and prayed. At the end of that prayer meeting not one of them was in doubt. The answer had to be yes. Phase One alone would cost £68,000 (the figure grew to £150,000). How it could ever be accomplished, God only knew!

Douglas Malton remembers very vividly the day that he and John went to the Foreign Office. By one of those extraordinary coincidences that, in retrospect, seem so perfect in their timing, the Wednesday they went — their only free time during the conference — was the one day when the official they needed to see was in his office for a work session between two stretches of leave. That very same day, they took delivery of an anxiously awaited file that was almost essential for backing up their request. This was a detailed study of what would be involved in setting up a Christian radio station, prepared originally by FEBA–Australia in connection with the Cocos Islands scheme, and accidentally left in Hong Kong by John!

It was an encouraging interview. They were advised to go straight to the Seychelles authorities supported by a letter from the Foreign Office. But a visit, it was then decided, would be even better than a letter. So the letter included a request that a representative might talk things over and offer fuller explanations to the Seychelles administration about the franchise they were seeking. The obvious person to go was John Wheatley.

Thousands of miles away in Manila, Alice, immersed in her daily work and the care of her family, was summoned suddenly to the phone. Would she join John in Bombay to catch the monthly boat to the Seychelles? Somehow she managed it in time! It made good sense to include a woman in this initial visit, for the men might easily have negotiated and planned without recognising the problems that would face wives and families. Not without misgivings, the Wheatleys stepped off the boat at Victoria. They had a fortnight on Mahé (until the boat returned) to approach responsible officials and review the situation.

The idea of establishing a new radio station was well received. The administration was very conscious of the need to increase international awareness of the Seychelles, and also to create new jobs for the Seychellois. Whereas the Australian authorities had spent five *years* considering whether to allow a station to be established in the Cocos Islands (and had still not announced a decision), it took the Seychelles administration three months to give outline permission, subject to certain basic conditions about location and similar matters. The same week, an answer came from Australia — there could be no station in the Cocos Islands.

By late August John was back on Mahé finalising arrangements with the government and surveying for land with the hope of getting an option on a suitable site before news of the airport and other development could set prices soaring. But his time was limited. Soon he had to move on to Britain and help FEBA in setting up the project, a process that involved many consultations and innumerable meetings of the Council. Bob Bowman came from Whittier, California, to discuss the relationship between FEBA and its parent FEBC. As the autonomy of FEBA was worked out, John Wheatley was released from his FEBC commitments and designated Field Director of FEBA. His scheduled three-week visit stretched to three months.

Finally, at a press conference on October 1, 1967, the Far Eastern Broadcasting Association announced its existence and its intentions. A limited company, it had a managerial Council consisting of all the men of the original Associates' committee. The Associates, now far more numerous, were the shareholders, paying nothing for their 'shares' but (in accordance with English company law) being liable to the extent of £1 should the company be forced into liquidation.

The history of missionary work is not always the story of men and women called in startling and dramatic ways to leave home and loved ones for the far corners of the earth. Christians go to foreign parts for all sorts of reasons, not least in the course of their everyday work.

Arthur Tuck was an engineer, in charge of the construction of the Rochon dam, one of several building projects in progress on Mahé just before and during the establishment of the FEBA radio station. Among these were the airport, an extended harbour and an American satellite tracking station. Arthur and his family had been there for two years, so he knew the island and its people. The fact that he was already on the spot proved invaluable for FEBA.

John met Arthur on his second visit to Mahé when he was unable to finalise the buying of a site because the Civil Aviation Authority had not yet approved the preferred aerial site. The decision was announced while John was in the UK and the letter arrived on a day when the FEBA Council was to meet. The time had come to launch the project. But the treasurer reported a balance of only £1,000, a mere fraction of what would be needed to buy the necessary land, let alone start building. Choosing to exercise faith rather than caution, the Council decided to cable Arthur Tuck asking him to buy land for housing and offices, if possible on a hillside near the transmitter site. In fact, while John was in Mahé he had unofficially inspected a possible site which was likely to come on the market and he wanted Arthur to make further enquiries about this.

The cable was never sent. On the day the Council met, Arthur cabled the news that a suitable plot was for sale, advertised in the *Seychelles Bulletin*. It proved to be the very site John had inspected. Should Arthur enter into negotiations, he asked? There could be no doubt about the answer!

It was remarkable that the land should be advertised at all. At that time business was not often done in this way. Early in the morning vendors would settle on the wall near the clock tower in the centre of Victoria. Along would come other businessmen and there and then they negotiated. One property developer used his mini-moke for an office.

Title and possession of the land were obtained in January 1968. John returned to Manila to arrange for the family move, then visited Australia where he encouraged the FEBC Council there to support the project, an interest they were now happy to pursue since there was no future in developing a base in the Cocos Islands. Malcolm and Maureen Fidge shortened a furlough and on the way back to India stayed on Mahé to keep an eye on things and get housing construction started until the Wheatleys and others arrived and work began in earnest.

At this point it may be helpful to outline very simply the needs of a radio station. First, the workers must have somewhere to live. If the station is situated in or near a large town, this may be no problem. Even so there are advantages in living fairly close together and near the station buildings. The land purchased for FEBA was on a hillside at Sans Souci, one and a half miles south-west of Victoria, the island's only town, some 700 feet up, with views out over the ocean and the small island opposite. On this sloping 14-acre site eight houses and five flats went up in the course of the next five years.

Second, there must be studios. Basically a studio is a room that has been soundproofed (thick door, walls and floor covered with sound-absorbent material, windows blocked, double-glazed or non-existent) so that the programmes made within it will be free from unwanted noise. But the broadcaster will not be alone in the studio. Somebody must put the programme on tape or see that it is going to the transmitter as it should. The equipment and staff needed for this are housed in a control room adjoining the studio and linked to it by a large window and an audio system for two-way conversations (hand-signals during transmission). Here the engineers control the volume and quality of the sounds and use a mixer to add pre-recorded music or the voice of the announcer to complete the programme.

Just above the houses at Sans Souci, directly on the winding road from Victoria, stands the studio building. Perched on the hillside, it now contains three studios and administration offices. It is air-conditioned against the tropical heat and humidity, a benefit not only to people working in the studios, but especially to the library with its racks and shelves of tapes and discs.

The third essential is a transmitter. This uses electric power (anything from 250 watts to one million watts or more in broadcasting work), in order to change the signal from the studio into 'waves' of energy capable of travelling varying distances (depending among other factors on the power used, the wave length and the terrain it passes over). The transmitter building on Mahé is situated on the coast five miles by road from the studio, down and round sixty or so bends, through the capital and out on the other side, at Anse Etoile.

Last, though by no means least, is the aerial. Essentially an aerial is a length of wire providing the transmitter with a springboard to 'bounce' the signal into space. In practice it is likely to be an extremely complex structure. The design of the aerial is critical. It must be capable of focusing the output from the transmitter and sending it all (or as much of it as possible) in one direction. Consider the difference between a fountain and a fire hose. A 'fountain' aerial would disperse the signal generally in all directions. A 'fire hose' aerial makes it possible to concentrate and focus the signal on a specific area. Thus at the end of a programme from Mahé to India, the aerial array may be adjusted by means of a system of switches, so that it is beamed towards East Africa, the area for the next broadcast. A good aerial, like a good fire hose, increases the strength of the signal, so that a 25 kilowatt transmitter may have its output increased to 1,000 kilowatts at the centre of the beam.

Building such an array involves a good deal of construction work. This was scheduled for a later stage. At first a temporary aerial, looking more like an overgrown TV aerial than anything else, was sited at Sans Souci, so that test transmissions could start as soon as possible, with the 2–3 kilowatt transmitter. Later a small antennae system (to use the technical term) was erected on the beach at Anse Etoile, fed from a 25–30 kilowatt transmitter, adequate for broadcasting into India and even Pakistan. Later still the FEBA team were to tackle a unique civil engineering assignment.

One of the most remarkable aspects of the Seychelles story is the way in which men and women with certain skills and experience became available at the right time just when they were needed. Those who support FEBA will find this no accident. It's just what might be expected, they will say, of God, the divine personnel manager. It is obviously not possible to mention everyone, but the stories of a few, here and there, will be of interest.

Graham Beggs, a builder from Ireland, was working in Johannesburg for the SAGM and had just completed a job. Uncertain what his next step should be, he prayed that if it was to work with FEBA, then some move would be made towards him. John Wheatley, in South Africa at the time, heard about Graham and went to see him. The result was that Graham left for Mahé in 1968. Eileen and the family followed in January 1969. Graham supervised the house and flat construction; Eileen took responsibility for book-keeping.

Also in January that year, Bob Twynham-Perkins, an Australian, was seconded by the International Christian Fellowship of India, where he had considerable experience of construction work. Leaving his Scottish wife with their family in Glasgow, he came to supervise the erection of the transmitter building at Anse Etoile.

Calvin Niebling looked after the beginning of the work in the studio. An Australian, he left wife, family and business for six strenuous months, during which his experience in building, electrical work and electronics proved invaluable. He was typical of many who were to come to Mahé for short periods for a specific purpose. The building was but a shell when the six months were ended and another builder was urgently needed.

His name was Don Wickens. He lived at Walton-on-Thames in Surrey where he was the hardworking director of a building company. Among the members of the church Don and Audrey Wickens attended was Joan Dorney, for many years a church-goer, but only two years into a personal experience of Christ. Widowed, with a married daughter, Joan says she reacted to her new-found faith with all the enthusiasm of a schoolgirl. What could she do at fifty-three? First she helped with the clerical work connected with all the buying FEBA had to do in those days. When a secretary was needed on Mahé, Joan volunteered and was accepted by the candidates' board, originally for a year. She went out in July and completed two three-year terms as John Wheatley's personal secretary before her retirement in 1976.

As he prepared to go to Joan's farewell service, Douglas hoped to meet Don Wickens. Perhaps from his wide circle of acquaintances he could suggest someone to undertake the studio building. But Don was not there and Douglas went away disappointed.

However Audrey Wickens was at the service, where she

heard about the various needs. Someone must replace Joan in the buying department and a man was needed for the studio. Having offered to help one evening a week with the secretarial work, she went home and asked her husband: 'How about going out to Seychelles for a year with FEBA to build the studio?' It was as well that it was her idea for if Don went Audrey would be left coping with the home and family on her own.

Don was not unwilling, but the obstacles seemed insurmountable. His company might not wish to release him; he was well into his fifties and might not pass a medical. They talked and prayed and decided that if he was given leave and pronounced fit enough, they would take it he was meant to go.

Joan had not been on the island a couple of months before Don joined her. Just under a year later he managed to get back for his son's graduation in Bradford — with twenty-four hours to spare.

This wasn't Don's only short-term stay. Staff shortages brought him back again in 1974 for the Australian-financed extensions to the studio, when he was able to see the project completed. But his second stay was not without incident. When he departed in 1975, he left behind on Mahé not only a solid building, but also his appendix. Later he returned, with his wife and daughter, but heart trouble brought his stay to an end in 1977.

The pioneers of 1968–9 began their work living in quite primitive conditions on an island which at that time was comparatively unknown and inaccessible. They were separated from the outside world (apart from a Cable and Wireless link) by thousands of miles of water. Ships came from England every six to eight weeks and, as we have already noted, from India and to and from Mombasa once a month. Although husbands and fathers heard from wives and families through the weekly mail plane, they had little hope of returning quickly if an emergency arose. Many important foodstuffs such as meat and potatoes were liable to run out, another reason why the boats were eagerly awaited. At the start, food was a constant problem: what to buy, what to cook and how to keep it from going mouldy. (Once the houses were built, a fridge was installed in each home.)

Not least among these fervently anticipated cargoes were the supplies and equipment for the construction. Life was not easy, but members of the FEBA team remember the close relationship and bond of affection that united them all.

They ripped out great roots undisturbed for centuries, cleared undergrowth, drilled and blasted rock, built roads, using all their skills — and especially their ingenuity — to the full. Even the apparently straightforward task of shifting supplies from the ship to the site called for resourcefulness and hard work. They were, by force of circumstances, do-it-yourself experts. In 1968 for example, 8,000 board feet of timber arrived from Singapore. 'It was not possible to have it pressure treated before shipment, so we have built a 25 foot long bath from sheet metal and have soaked all the timber in preservative, much quicker and more thorough than brushing.' So runs that year's report. There was plenty of scope for improvisation.

Some items were late arriving and this meant the frustration of work held up while they waited. Sometimes vital machinery or equipment broke down and there was no means of getting it repaired on Mahé. At this point Arthur Tuck comes into the story again — but in a new and remarkable role. After leaving Mahé in February 1968, he took a job in England. This however did not last as long as he expected and, having again changed employment, he found himself in — of all places — Mombasa, the port on the east coast of Africa used by the steamer service to and from Seychelles. So far as FEBA was concerned Arthur was, once more, the right man in the right place.

Very often he could personally attend at the docks when cargo needed clearing. On one occasion, when the test transformer broke down, and was sent out on the good ship *Nord-*

vaer, Arthur met it at Mombasa, had it transferred to the port electrician's office, repaired and reloaded on the same ship for its next sailing.

His prompt assistance saved FEBA from being off the air for weeks. In fact Arthur Tuck became so involved with FEBA that he ultimately joined as a full-timer and supervised the Phase Two aerial construction two years later. But during Phase One he was far more useful in Mombasa.

At the start, the 3-kilowatt transmitter was housed with other necessary equipment in the first flat built. This accommodation was crowded but sufficient until studio and transmitter buildings were complete. The first aerial went up on the hill top, enabling test transmissions to start on October 18, 1969. On January 5 this test period was extended from six to eight hours. By the end of February 1970, 178 letters had been received from the reception area and 78 from other countries. It was not a very impressive response, but it did mean that just two years after the formation of FEBA, the small transmitter in this tiny island in the middle of the Indian Ocean was beaming a signal into the subcontinent.

Successful though the test operation had been, a bigger transmitter was needed. FEBC offered a spare 30-kilowatt model and in June 1969 it reached Mahé. With it came David Bacon and his wife Brenda. As early as 1963 David had discussed his career with Douglas Malton. Considerable experience with Marconi's following his PhD studies in cosmic ray research and a spell at Bible College (where he met Brenda) meant that he was just ready to join FEBA as one of its first transmitter engineers. He went to supervise the shipment of the Manila model, met delay in getting it out of the country and so was able to familiarise himself with it. On Mahé the machine was installed and operational by April 1970.

The new programme schedule demanded more staff. In 1970 Geoffrey and Eileen Cook arrived on Mahé, with their four daughters, where he became programme director. Geoff's past experience included a science degree at Glasgow, work as an army officer, and in industry and teaching. He was already interested in Christian radio when he went to the Moody Bible Institute, where he had studio experience and gained a Pastor's Diploma. Since there was at that time no vacancy at HCJB with whom he had hoped to serve, he returned to the UK and spent eight years with a Christian recording studio before joining FEBA. He took over from Alice Wheatley, whose Manila experience was invaluable once transmissions from Mahé began.

Kay Seager, who also arrived in 1970, had several years' experience with the BBC. She no longer appears under this name in the FEBA list; in 1971 Kay married John Claridge, who had gone to Mahé as a studio engineer.

Everyone looked forward to May 10, 1970, the date when the new station was to be 'officially' on the air. This would mark the end of test transmissions, the commencement of the new programme schedules.

Among the routine preliminaries before the big day was checking the purity of the hundreds of gallons of oil which cool the transformers. A sample had been sent to laboratories in Kenya for testing, a precaution prior to putting high voltages through the transformers. When the report came back, ironically on April 1, it gave the technical staff a nasty shock – but not so much of a shock as they would have had if the current had been fed into the transformers. The chemical content of the oil had in fact 'gone bad'! With only four weeks to go before being on the air the old oil would have to be drained down, the cores and windings lifted out for cleaning, the tanks scrubbed and replacement oil obtained. 'Our emotions were mixed between disgust at such a horrible job and gratitude to God that we had not been permitted to put full power on the transformer,' wrote John Wheatley.

The operation would have been pretty formidable in England – but in the Seychelles . . .! The first problem was the removal of the central cores, the two largest weighing 1½ tons each. Normally a mobile crane could have done the job but as the transmitter building was by then substantially complete, there was no way to get a crane in. So in four days FEBA staff built their own two-ton crane out of old angle iron and hoisted the parts 12 feet high for cleaning. Scrubbing brushes were needed to shift the thick layer of brown crystalline salt – a deposit which had come out of the oil. David Bacon was the one who, in that sticky humidity, climbed into the drained-down 300-gallon tank to scrub the inside.

While all this was going on, a search was being made throughout Mahé for fresh oil – a very special grade not readily available on a remote island. Thirteen drums were needed. One drum was supplied by Shell who suggested their associated company in East Africa might be able to help. The shipping company revealed that a boat that would take inflammable cargo was just then loading in Mombasa. An urgent cable to Arthur Tuck who contacted the Shell representative resulted in six more drums being found and transferred to the ship in the nick of time.

Six drums were still required. As a result of previous enquiries on the island, the airport contractors phoned to say they had found at the back of a shed and covered with tarpaulin six drums of the right kind of oil for which they had no use, 'and didn't know why they had been ordered'. So the 'on the air' schedule was fulfilled.

Thus after two and a half years of sweat, toil and prayer, with Phase One complete, on July 6 the staff and a hundred guests watched His Excellency the Governor of Seychelles, Sir Bruce Greatbatch, cut the strands of recording tape tied across the main door of the studio building for the opening ceremony.

CHAPTER 4

Building on the Rock

FEBA HAD ACHIEVED its immediate aim of broadcasting to India and Pakistan. Reception was good in South India but further north it became less clear. To reach into northernmost India as well as the Middle East and Southern Asia, to say nothing of East Africa which was nearer but in a different direction, bigger aerials and a more powerful transmitter were needed. As early as 1967 plans had been laid for the next chapter of the FEBA Seychelles story.

Offshore from the beach at Anse Etoile, and about 4,000 feet out, there is a coral reef. Masts erected here (and some would need to be 300 feet tall) would be far enough out and sufficiently high to send a signal over the heights of Mahé Island. There was no adequate alternative site on the island itself. Phase Two, the Reef Aerial Project (RAP) was given the go-ahead in January 1971. It offered the FEBA engineers the distinction of planning and putting into operation the first enterprise of its kind ever undertaken. Pioneering days were not over yet!

A thousand square yards of foreshore in front of the transmitter building at Anse Etoile were reclaimed for establishing workshops and a slipway. Machinery was assembled. A tug, work boats, pontoons and a dredger were acquired. The principal work boat, a flat-bottomed barge-like craft specially shipped out from England was bought with a £3,000 gift from the London Emmanuel Choir in memory of its founder and conductor, Edwin Shepherd. It was his widow, Muriel, who launched the craft in Newhaven Harbour, naming it *Emmanuel*. Backwards and forwards it went in the waters of the reef, towing and carrying men and materials from the shore to the reef site.

Months of planning, surveying and paper work could not eliminate all the problems and practical difficulties. What follows may appear rather technical and complicated at times, but it is offered, not to confound the simple-minded (and the writer was left feeling very confused — even after explanations and after having seen it all!) but as a tribute to consecrated skill and hard work and as a record of a quite remarkable achievement.

The first problem was how to excavate the holes up to 10 feet below the surface in the hard coral bed. These were needed as solid bases for the masts and the stilt-like columns on which the switch-house would be perched, and for anchor points to which wires supporting the masts would be attached. In addition 5,000 feet of trench must be dug to house the power and control cables which went out to the mast lights and aerial switches.

On paper it looked deceptively simple to lower the suction pipe of the dredger to the reef and suck away the sand and coral rubble until there was a suitably sized pit for the concrete foundations. But once on the job the dredger intake pipe was blocked within minutes by chunks of broken coral and the flow ceased. So two divers had to remain at the intake for the sole function of keeping the pipe cleared and flowing. With iron bars they would prod the impacted lumps of coral to keep them moving up the pipe.

Byrd Brunemeier and his eighteen-year-old son were both involved in this early dredging work. The family had come out to Mahé for a short period to help. As he stood in the murky waters, his hands lacerated from the razor-sharp coral, Byrd was heard to comment that no *money* in all the world would have tempted him into such an uncomfortable situation. 'I did it for the Lord of the harvest and for the millions of India who were without Christ.' Yet this was no final solution. The 'bite-at-a-time' method was taking two weeks to excavate each pit. There must be some other way to avoid this tedious and painful underwater labour.

Arthur Tuck, now working full time for FEBA, designed a mechanical boring and crushing device, motor driven, which, together with a hydraulically powered excavator (specially shipped out from Britain, putting an unexpected £2,000 on the RAP bill) coped with the coral. The excavator was mounted on a pontoon. Visibility from the cab was limited so the driver positioned his bucket by using an ingenious system of 'sights' set up by the Site Engineer doing the surveying. Then in those murky, stirred-up waters the Site Engineer would check whether the hole was the correct size. Happily, throughout this period workers escaped one serious potential danger. No-one came into contact with the spikes carried by a poisonous fish that inhabits those waters.

Another short-term worker who had brought his wife and family out at this time was Don McLeod. The RAP confirmed his belief that when God wants a man to do a job he very often trains him in advance. While working in his native Scotland Don found himself unexpectedly transferred to an assignment that a colleague had previously been responsible for: underwater surveying for landing stages, piers and bridges on the islands of the Inner Hebrides. A keen radio 'ham', Don had wondered whether he should offer to help on Mahé.

One morning he went downstairs early and found TWR were relaying a 'Back to the Bible' broadcast featuring special missionary needs all over the world. FEBA's need for an experienced civil engineer for underwater surveying was mentioned. The tape had been made six months before, but it confirmed Don's half-formed intention. He was soon out on Mahé using his recently acquired expertise in the waters of the coral reef.

The story of how FEBA acquired part of the lattice mast material for the RAP presents a further example of celestial serendipity. In 1969 the US government satellite tracking station had contracted out a special job, the provision of several antennae complete with masts. The contractor had installed masts and aerials but failed to meet the high standard of performance demanded in the contract. So he abandoned it. Masts and other material were simply dismantled and stacked in a dump of surplus material. Later the equipment was put up for sale. But who could possibly need these massive metal lattices? Thus it was at an absurd price, below the cost of scrap iron, that FEBA was able to purchase the bulk of the reef aerial masts — and two miles of submersible control cable.

Supplementing and facilitating all this work on Mahé was a great deal of activity in England. As requests came through for items, as machinery broke down and calls for help were received at the Woking office, so a tremendous network of contacts developed to supply and assist. One among many was a plant hire firm sympathetic to the aim of FEBA's work, through whom sound and often carefully vetted second-hand equipment was procured at the most reasonable prices available. They responded splendidly to emergencies too. Even the best machinery could not take the strain of some of the operations. Twice the sleeve of the excavator had to be completely rebuilt on the island. But a broken crankshaft on the concrete mixing platform was not so easily dealt with. On the Friday when disaster struck, the news and the catalogue number of the broken part were cabled to Woking. The plant hire firm used business contacts to track down a replacement. This was delivered to Woking, hurriedly packed and taken to the airport. It reached Mahé on Sunday. Monday morning saw it through the customs and the workshop staff took until midnight reassembling the diesel engine with the new crankshaft. By Tuesday the concreting operation was in business as usual.

Employees of Costains, the giant civil engineering company also (!) working on Mahé, were frankly incredulous that a machine which broke down on Friday on an island in the middle of the Indian Ocean could be operational again by

Tuesday. But for FEBA it was not only time that was important. Every day cost money, whether they were working or not.

The drama unfolding on Mahé required massive support behind the scenes in the United Kingdom. At the very beginning and during the Phase One construction, the scene of some of the most intense activity had been the house of Malcolm Clough. Chief buyer for a big company, his experience not only helped in procuring the vast number of items needed, but his home became the warehouse and packing station. For over two years he and his long-suffering wife lived amongst consignments of everything from nuts and bolts to lengths of plastic sanitary piping, awaiting the volunteers who came to pack and load supplies on to the van which drove to Tilbury Docks to catch one of the infrequent boats to Seychelles.

Then the operation was moved to Woking where Audrey Wickens, who had taken Joan Dorney's place at the Cloughs, was glad to have the further help of FEBA Council members some of whom had come to live in the area in order to assist.

During the RAP work, the Woking office dealt with 700 orders in addition to the normal work load. Things were not made any easier by the tendency of telegrams to garble messages, as when 'drawing No. B.19 not received' became 'drawing No. B.19 not *required*'.

Four thousand tons of reinforced concrete were needed to complete the bases on the reef. Next the masts had to be erected. A hoist pulley rigged into place slowly raised the 20-foot panels one by one to the required height. Engineers who had been splashing around in the Indian Ocean now found themselves hanging perilously aloft as, section upon section, the masts grew towards the sky. Next the wire curtain had to be fixed. It was prepared on land and towed by pontoon into the sea where a top cable hoisted it into position and the lower elements were added stage by stage. Neil Wescombe supervised and worked on many of the RAP operations with skill and with a particular personal satisfaction. He joined the FEBA team in June 1971 as a mechanical and construction engineer.

With his wife Ruth he had spent four years with a mission in India. He appreciated, as one who had lived in the subcontinent and heard FEBC broadcasts, how much the new station would mean to its people. So he was particularly glad to be playing a practical part in providing the stronger signal and therefore greater scope for the radio ministry whose effectiveness he already warmly believed in.

September 1973 saw the arrival of the eagerly awaited new transmitter, a Gates SW-100, and the beginning of a long chapter of faith-testing and frustration. Newly developed, it was of very high efficiency, but because FEBA bought the production development model they paid less than 40 per cent the normal price. Familiar problems made a fresh appearance. Parts were broken during shipment and replacements were ordered immediately. When they came in February 1974 installation began at once. Permission to use it was sought and granted, but not at full power. Its maximum output needed special clearance. Since the inception of the Reef Aerial Project, the flight path of aircraft approaching Mahé had been changed so that there was now a risk that radiation from the powerful transmitter via the massive aerial array might endanger landing planes because of interference to communications frequencies and radio navigational aids. Tests must be made to ensure that no such interference was possible.

The remoteness of the islands, the limited facilities available and the lack of special expertise meant that the government could not work out the detailed specification for the tests, let alone carry them out. The consequent delay and uncertainty dragged on for more than three years and tried both patience and faith. Six months of negotiations in London produced a test specification. FEBA engineers then procured a special meter and ran some tests of their own. They did not doubt that some work must be done: filters must be designed and built to reduce interference and arrangements made for screening the transmitter building. The latter had narrow slits cut in the floor to house copper strips. The machine for cutting was not only deafening; the dust raised by it choked everyone. Ingenuity, however, again won the day. Within a few hours a triumphant Don Wickens was pushing his machine along, just as noisy, but with a handsome hood over the hole that was spitting out the dust.

Designing and constructing the filters was another matter. Two months of calculation were needed, even with the help of an electronic calculator. During the winter months of 1974–5 Brenda (especially) and David Bacon shivered on furlough while a Hewlett Packard calculator followed the instructions David fed into it — day and night. Time was short. The work had to be finished in time for tests scheduled for April 1975 involving a specially equipped aircraft which was to fly through the radio 'beam'.

Returning to Mahé with some of his homework done, David Bacon unexpectedly found help close at hand. When called in to rectify a breakdown in the computer at a government office in Victoria, he took the opportunity of asking whether it could ever be available for him. Certainly, he was told, outside of working hours. Making use of this machine saved days of calculations.

Although the tests were postponed to June, there were other problems. Transmitter valves kept failing and spares ran out, for instance. Replacements arrived in time and the special tests took place on June 18–19. Further faults in the transmitter even during those two days called for quick action; and no-one expected the main electricity supply cable to catch fire and explode!

There were still more months of delay while the aviation report went through to the Foreign and Commonwealth Office to be ultimately relayed through diplomatic channels to the Seychelles government, who at that time had more than enough on their hands. For in October 1975 the Seychelles became internally self-governing and the islands celebrated Independence Day on June 29, 1976. FEBA also had their celebrations about the same time. Permission to work the transmitter at maximum power and use the new reef aerials to the full had been granted, initially for six months while the final ratification process could be worked out.

However, at 2 a.m. on Sunday June 5, 1977, President Mancham's government was deposed in an almost bloodless coup and was replaced by a new government, headed by the former Prime Minister, Albert Rene. At first FEBA continued to broadcast normally but later was asked to discontinue for 'security reasons' and went off the air for a total of nineteen days. This period of silence left no room for uncertainty about the popularity of the programmes. Letters flooded in to Delhi, Bangalore and Mahé asking for an explanation of the silence, expressing sympathy and a sense of loss, promising fasting and prayer with a view to the recommencement of the broadcasts.

Following the nineteen days of silence, permission was given to broadcast at up to 50 kilowatts. The new President gave an assurance that the attitude of the new government towards FEBA was no different from that of the previous one and that they were welcome in the island.

1977 turned out, in fact, to be a year of unprecedented difficulty. Illness and accident struck time and again, and for one reason or another, individuals and families — many with years of service — had to leave Mahé. And 1978 saw no easing of the problems. But there were two encouraging developments. An increasing number of young people showed interest in working on Mahé. And the new government reaffirmed its willingness to co-operate with FEBA. At the time of writing, negotiations are still continuing for a licence to broadcast up to peak power of 100 kilowatts.

CHAPTER 5

Life on Mahé

MANY PEOPLE HAVE only the vaguest concept of what being 'a missionary' means in practice. Thousands who support the work of FEBA Seychelles by praying and giving have become familiar with place-names such as Mahé, Victoria and Sans Souci through constantly reading of them in prayer letters. But they can't imagine what it is like to live on Mahé. This chapter may help to give a realistic impression of what is involved in Christian radio work in one particular situation.

'Picture turquoise calm waters shaded by casuarina trees and coconut palms, bordered by lovely stretches of soft white coral sands. Picture the most spectacular and varied marine scenery in the world — this is the Seychelles.' So speaks the tour operator's advertisement! Certainly the beauty of Mahé impresses the visitor from the first moment when it is seen rising towards the descending aeroplane from out of the glittering Indian Ocean. On the quieter less populated side of the island the sands are almost unbelievably white and you can have an entire beach to yourself for an afternoon. A narrow coastal road winds its way round most of the island. Other roads cut across at five or six places. The central highland reaches 3,000 feet, almost as high as Snowdon, so those roads rise and fall steeply, offering breathtaking views not only of areas of Mahé itself, but beyond to some of its nearer neighbours in the group. Mahé houses 85 per cent of the total Seychelles population. The rest are scattered over a few of the remaining islands (Seychelles totals *in all* about 171 square miles) such as Praslin, La Digue and Silhouette.

The naturalist and the historian will find plenty of interest in Mahé. The French names are a reminder of that nation's exploration and rule in the eighteenth century before the Seychelles finally capitulated to Britain in 1804. Seychelles was a dependency of the Mauritius Crown Colony until 1903, when it became a Crown Colony in its own right. The inhabitants, originally settlers, slaves and traders, come from Europe, Africa, Madagascar, China and India. The result is that most of them have coloured skins and many have European features. The influence of French language, culture and outlook, combined with some pride in British nationality (just come to an end) and deep attachment to Roman Catholicism provide the sociologist too with some fascinating material.

The naturalist may study 3,000 or more species of land animals (mostly insects) and the remains of what was once a unique vegetation, not least the palms, including the famous coco-de-mer. This remarkably shaped coconut was suspected by General Gordon to have been the original tree of the knowledge of good and evil in the Garden of Eden. Among the animals is the giant tortoise, which can reach five feet in length and weigh as much as 500 pounds.

Another newspaper item recommending the Seychelles as a holiday resort is a little more honest. It hints that this paradise (and it has been called a 'forgotten Eden'), even if it has no serpent in it, suffers from at least some disadvantages. A cautious reference to 'unspoilt places where the sun is almost certain to shine and the people nearly always smile' should be noted by those who imagine the FEBA team at work and play and think how nice it must be to serve the Lord on a tropical island. 'The qualifications are necessary,' the article continues, 'because . . . the Seychelles are not a winter sun paradise — December and January can be very wet.' This is certainly true. At its most torrential, the rain has an alarming habit of washing down pathways so that they become miniature rivers. The little colony at Sans Souci experienced this on their steep hill-side. In the end money had to be spared to concrete the roads linking the houses.

Yet the rain brings welcome refreshment. Although the temperature on Mahé rarely rises above 32 C° or falls below 22°C, the relative humidity *averages* 75–80 per cent all the year round and can reach as high as 95 per cent. The equable temperature means you can wear the lightest of summer clothing, but the hot moist atmosphere leaves you longing to shed even that *and* a layer or two of skin as well . . . A climate such as this is bearable for tourists who lounge lazily on the beach or in a hotel, but it drains the energies of anybody who has to do a day's work. At the end of two years, FEBA staff are ready for three months home leave, if they can get away. After three years, when they can have six months furlough, their overall vitality, to say nothing of their efficiency, can be quite seriously impaired.

In a climate like this air-conditioning is no luxury! In the radio station's record and tape library it is essential. To enter the room is like walking into a refrigerator. Why are the tapes thus favoured? Because they will soon go mouldy, whereas human beings are tougher, and can endure it without relief although not in the studios or control rooms which are kept at a lower temperature.

An unexpected effect of the climate is the length of time needed for a wound to heal. Germs thrive in humid conditions and even a scratch can remain open and raw for some days. Although the Seychelles are free from diseases that afflict many tropical countries — malaria, yellow fever or cholera — residents do not escape such irritations as coughs and colds, or even flu and bronchitis. All the same, during 1977 the work of FEBA was seriously affected by an epidemic of dengue fever which struck at many of the workers.

Like the climate, the wild life on the island can be endured if you are not too fussy and keep your house scrupulously clean. You must not be worried by lizards that dart suddenly across your walls and shed their tail if you grab them; fat, furry spiders, the size of a clenched fist can be seen, happily not indoors, but attached to webs suspended on structures such as telegraph poles and wires; cockroaches and ants find their way into all sorts of unexpected places. So do some other creatures. On one well remembered and often recounted occasion a lizard got into the shirt of one of the studio operators. The programme going out during this transmission was live. As the announcer watched his unhappy Seychellois colleague's contortions, he gave the audience a moment by moment account of how the operator was coping. Liz Scott, who joined the team on Mahé after some free-lance experience with Radio Voice of the Gospel, Ethiopia, found herself wondering what to do with a fly which settled persistently on her nose, while she was announcing. If she blew it away the amplified sound might have startled her listeners. To squash it would have been messy. The programme director's subsequent advice was that she should have swallowed it!

Yet another adjustment for those who go to live on a tropical island (and Mahé is only 300 miles from the equator) concerns food. Victoria, the only town on the island, has several modern supermarkets, but nothing like a local High Street with its variety of shops, including an old-fashioned grocer and perhaps a delicatessen, to cater for all tastes. Most foods (and none are prepacked) can be available in Mahé at a price and as long as stocks last. But sometimes there is a six-month wait for an item and such 'essentials' as sugar, flour, margarine or dried milk may be out of stock for several weeks. The market is the best place, naturally, for local-grown vegetables and fruits — bananas (there are about 30 varieties in the Seychelles) pineapples, mangoes, limes, breadfruit, egg plant, cassava and that delightful cross between an orange and a grapefruit — the pomela. As the day wears on and if the sea has not been too rough, the boats return with fish, the basic Seychellois diet. It is quite usual to see people walking through the streets in late afternoon carrying their purchases — an octopus, or a fish up to two feet long — on a string.

But even when you have learned to name and recognise the unfamiliar local produce, you may not know what to do with it. What some regard as exciting or even humorous gastronomic discoveries may be purgatory for more tender digestions and less adventurous dispositions!

And food costs money. In this respect the FEBA housewife has an even tougher job than her British sister because of the effects of inflation on a cost of living which has always been higher than in Europe. FEBA living allowances have risen with prices, in fact they have doubled since 1970, and while no fear of redundancy can hang over the FEBA worker, yet he cannot earn more money with overtime, nor can his wife take a job to bring in extra. The money just has to stretch.

It is perhaps relevant at this point to recognise the impact of tourism. The 1971 Annual Report of FEBA summed up the dramatic development during that year in which the airport became operational. The opening of new hotels led to food shortages and the beginning of inflationary prices. The somewhat erratic water supply became even more uncertain during periods of drought as tourism made increasing demands. Provision for visitors has continued to figure largely in the islands' growth. Tourism is the third biggest employer. Plans for future development are based on an estimated 100,000 visitors per year by 1980 — as many as the estimated population at the end of the century. FEBA families were affected when trained house girls turned to the new hotels for employment and the shortage of capable workers in responsible or technical jobs was aggravated by the attraction of other concerns that offered inflated wages. The rapid rate of change in the years since 1971 has left the older Seychellois quite lost. More than ever there is a glaring contrast between the tin shacks and tiny homes of some of the islanders and the splendour of some of the newly constructed, air-conditioned buildings.

In one respect FEBA families are perhaps better off than they would be in Britain, especially the younger ones. Some at least would not live in such roomy houses as those on the airy hillside at Sans Souci, or the two by the sea at Anse Etoile. The three-bedroomed houses are all basically on the same pattern. Some are on one floor, others on two. The main living area is open plan. The kitchen is a good size and well equipped. These might be in a western home, were it not for the filter on the tap, the green mesh at the windows and the huge ceiling fan set to rotate at varying speeds depending on the temperature. Although other jobs are increasingly available, some Seychellois women and girls are willing to work as home helps. The FEBA wife who works many hours each day in studio or office finds them invaluable. The trusted girl can be housekeeper, washerwoman, cook and baby-minder as required. Some leave to have children. One of the social problems among the islanders is the high illegitimacy rate, of more than 40 per cent.

These homes provide a modestly furnished and comfortable base for relaxation after the day's work. At the transmitter station, the day begins at 4 a.m. when the equipment has to be 'warmed up' for the first transmission before 5 a.m. Ideally there should be four engineers manning the station in shifts, and another with sole responsibility for maintaining the aerials. But often only two men have been available and it has not been unknown for one person to be left in sole charge. At the other end of the day programmes are transmitted late into the evening. Weekends, far from being time off, are busiest of all. This is peak time for listeners in the reception areas who are themselves at leisure. In theory every staff member has two complete days off every week, but staffing shortages rarely permit this. Although four teams of Seychellois operators work in shifts, a missionary engineer must be on call to cope in an emergency. Sometimes an operator is off sick. Sometimes faults occur in the equipment. An emergency might mean a series of technical mishaps, one after the other. What is it like to live with this constant strain? Brenda Bacon with seven years' experience, writes: 'We never know what is just round the corner of course. In fact we live in a situation where at any time things could become too difficult for us to cope, but I believe the Lord keeps things in control to the extent that He has spared us this so far. It must be something to do with the prayers of folk back home.'

Most missionary members of the programme department do not start so early as their Anse Etoile colleagues. The earliest transmissions are supervised by Seychellois operators using pre-recorded tapes and cassettes in vernacular languages. The operator usually sleeps in the studio and relies on an alarm (or, failing that, the night watchman) to wake him. Again, a missionary member of the department has to be ready to be called should anything go wrong.

Otherwise the studio complex at Sans Souci comes alive at 8 a.m. The day starts with a staff prayer meeting which remembers not only local needs but those of others in similar situations around the world. The first 'live' programme goes out at 10.30 a.m. During the other English language transmissions a programmer is needed in the studio — and when not on duty in this way, the staff are preparing their items for other programmes. In this department, as for the engineers, evening and weekend duties occur more or less frequently and make more or less of a demand according to the number of people available.

It is preparing live programmes that imposes the main strain on the programmers. Apart from the need to decide what will appeal to the Indian audience, material must be drawn from whatever meagre sources are available. When one thinks of the BBC archives, built up over years, and all the library and other resources provided in London (let alone the rest of the country) and then compares these with the few reference books, the kindly donated *Encyclopaedia Britannica* and the magazines and papers sent by well-wishers, it is amazing what the programmers achieve.

When the day ends and duties are finished, the FEBA fathers and mothers, like parents anywhere, return home to devote themselves to the children or to household tasks. Father might even put his feet up and relax. Mother is less likely to be able to. FEBA wives are usually involved in radio work — in fact it is policy that they should be. Some jobs can be done at home, others take them to the radio station building. They prepare programmes, announce, check tapes, sort out items in the traffic department, answer letters and do many secretarial and administrative jobs. One prepares a monthly newsletter, another has even spent hours on circuit board wiring. Not least among their many responsibilities is the care of their husbands, seeing they get the food and sleep they need in a situation where, if one member is off, all are affected. There are no spares for replacement!

The children of school age attend the International School in Victoria. The older ones have to pass an entrance examination to gain places at the two government-aided (single sex) secondary schools. Here they can sit for Cambridge University Examination Board O levels. But the competition for these schools is intense and for those who do not pass the examination there is no alternative. This presents a very real problem for the families concerned.

Those of the FEBA family who live a bachelor existence return, like their counterparts all over the world, to the quietness and the sometimes loneliness of their homes. If they don't want to stay in for an evening or at the weekend on their own, they have to decide where to seek companionship and how to occupy the time. Some have friends among the Seychellois or other Europeans on the island. There are a limited number of activities: badminton, tennis and basketball, a monthly theatre club and a musical evening in a local home where folk gather just to enjoy singing and also to sing to others on special occasions. They go to the hospital at Christmas time. And there is always the beach and swimming.

Victoria, capital of Mahé, and the only town, doesn't provide much scope for outings. It is but a handful of streets. By reclaiming land from the sea, the port was enlarged so that ships could come close in. A single wide street of brand new shops leads down to the quay, with colourful mini-mokes parked by the roadside tempting visitors to see the island for themselves.

Dominating the centre of the town is the clock tower, one of its few main features, a reminder of earlier colonial days. Erected by public subscription in 1903 in memory of Queen Victoria, it is a small replica of the tower clock of London's Vauxhall Bridge Road. There are two cinemas, and a number of expensive restaurants. Not much for anyone seeking a break from FEBA routine, or an evening out!

The journey from the radio station and settlement on the Sans Souci hillside to Victoria is a somewhat hair-raising and dizzy descent. Estimates of the number of hairpin bends on the road vary, but there are at least sixty, and even in the coolest time of the year it is not a trip to be undertaken on foot. So most FEBA families have a middle-aged or elderly car for island travel. It was for the sake of these vehicles, as well as the conscientious or figure-conscious folk who walk, that those roads on the hillside had to be concreted. Usually at least one car goes up from the houses to the radio station first thing in the morning. People meet at a crossroads on the hillside familiarly known as Piccadilly Circus. But if you are not there when the car of the day swings momentarily into position, you walk up. It is not very arduous, though you may arrive puffing and hot at the top, if you are late or feeling energetic. On the whole, however, Mahé is not a place where you hurry anywhere if you can help it.

A car is certainly the quickest and most efficient way of getting between the studio and the transmitter station. Anse Etoile is a mile and a half beyond Victoria, going north, along the coast road. The transmitter building is almost on the beach. Whether you look out to sea at this point or survey the distant scene from the Sans Souci balconies, the imposing aerial array is a striking feature. On the inland side of the road where the hillside rises sharply, stand the two houses built for the engineers and their families. It was with enormous relief that they moved into these homes once they were completed in 1974. Living on top of their work may not be everybody's dream, but when an emergency call comes through an engineer can be called from his home, for he has only a narrow set of steps to negotiate, the road to cross, and he is on the job in a matter of minutes.

Because hours on duty vary and because of the distance between the two stations, FEBA staff have to meet as and when they can. They gather for prayer and study as well as to discuss business. The women meet fortnightly for coffee, sharing and Bible study. Once a month there is a combined communion service.

Before the Seychelles became British, French rule and settlers' influence had marked the island for only forty years but the bulk of the population is still nominally Roman Catholic. The Anglican St Paul's Cathedral in Victoria is the only Protestant place of worship. Here some of the FEBA workers worship, sing in the choir and help in the Sunday School. Others have for several years arranged a Sunday evening service, first in a house and more recently at the teachers' training college. It combines both worship and evangelistic outreach and has been the means of bringing a living personal faith to many Seychellois.

Although they are not allowed to broadcast to this 'parish on their doorstep', FEBA members have sought a ministry among their Seychellois neighbours, with whom they can be in personal contact, although so remote from those whom they try to reach over the air. A Bible study began by request in the home of someone who had moved to the quieter side of the island. A Chinese contact was linked with David Wong who, with his wife Alice, joined the FEBA team from Singapore. These are only two examples of many ways in which links are forged.

The other link is through work. Some of the Seychellois staff have been influenced by the witness of colleagues. One young man in particular is now working in the monitoring department in New Delhi having started his association with FEBA on Mahé. His family had been forced to return to Seychelles from Kenya, where he was brought up. Much against his parents' wishes he became a Christian, largely through hearing the programmes as they went out. He went to Bible college and married in India where he is now on the FEBAI Staff.

Life on Mahé has its tough side and its lighter touches, has its excitements and its frustrations but one thing is certain — there's never a dull moment.

CHAPTER 6

Getting it Together

WE TAKE SO many things for granted! Today's BBC Radio Four transmissions begin at 6.20 a.m. with the news headlines. By midnight and the end of the inshore waters weather forecast, 45 programmes will have taken the air. And somebody has had to take a decision about the whole enterprise. How many programmes? Which ones? In what order? For how long?

It's surprising how often listeners' grouches refer to programming. There's too much/too little sport/classical music/pop/hard rock/drama/current affairs. Religious programmes coincide with the times of church services so that a large proportion of potential listeners can't hear them. Serious talks are too late/too early in the evening. Why was that very crude comedy show placed just after the children's programme?

Few people realise that Christian radio also has programming problems. Perhaps the most obvious is the need to decide which languages to employ and at what times to broadcast. Audience research (which we shall mention later) is obviously important in this context. What languages are actually spoken by people living within range of the transmitter? When are they most likely to be listening?

In passing, it's worth pointing out that this question of timing presents a serious difficulty for Christian radio organisations which buy time on commercial transmitters. They are often limited to late night and early morning times that the commercial station is not particularly interested in because so few people are listening. Short-wave broadcasts, however, although perhaps transmitted in the early morning, may be heard, thousands of miles away, at very different times. Obviously the best way to secure prime time (that is, the time when most people listen) is either to find a station that will sell it — probably at a high price! — or else to provide a Christian station.

Programming is simplest where a small number of programmes are put out in each of several languages. Thus FEBA currently broadcasts in 19 languages besides English, with something like 224 15-minute programmes per week. Most of these (non-English) programmes are religious. The decisions to be taken are:

1. How to vary the type of programme (Bible exposition, magazine, drama, evangelistic message, 'hymn and a thing').
2. Whether to 'block' the time for each language, thus providing a continuous series of programmes, or to scatter the different programmes throughout the day or week (it may seem risky to put all your eggs in one basket, but missing — for whatever reason — five minutes of an *isolated* 15-minute programme means losing 30 per cent of that evening's listening).
3. What time to select, a decision complicated by the need to co-ordinate the most suitable times for various types of listener.

   When a bigger block of time is available (FEBA broadcasts in English to South Asia from 06.30 to 08.30 and 15.35 to 16.50 GMT on every weekday), the choices are more complex.
4. Most important, perhaps — should a Christian radio station transmit only religious programmes? Some people are shocked that the question should even be asked. Surely, they argue, it can't be right to take money given (often at personal sacrifice) for 'the Lord's work' and use it to broadcast news bulletins, magazine programmes and secular music. Such material never saved anybody's soul. In any

case, there is no shortage of secular stations for this purpose; why should Christians get involved?

So far as they go, these are sound arguments. But, interestingly, they are not generally accepted by Christian radio stations. HCJB was honoured by the government of Ecuador in 1955 for its social and cultural as well as its spiritual work. FEBC has been similarly recognised.

But why allocate scarce resources to programmes that seem to have no spiritual significance? The first answer is that the secular content attracts listeners who might not otherwise tune in. In order to evangelise, it is essential to attract a non-Christian audience. News bulletins and music are popular everywhere, so are programmes devoted to hobbies such as philately, numismatics, and DX-ing (listening to short-wave broadcasts). As an Ecuador army captain explained to a HCJB worker: 'Every morning, the first thing I do after I wake up is turn the radio on and tune in HCJB. I listen for the time signal so that I will not be late getting to my office. Then I listen to the news. I don't bother to read the newspapers, I just listen to HCJB. I know that what I hear there is true and reliable and the latest news available . . . Like most men, I am a little bit lazy at times. I turn my radio on to listen to the news. Then I get busy doing this and that, and I can't be bothered turning the thing off, so I end up by listening to your religious broadcasts . . . there is absolutely nothing wrong with them . . . and the fact of the matter is, Señores, as I have listened, I have really learned to like them.'

From India comes a similar statement: 'Through one of my friends, I got introduced to FEBA, only very recently, and to my surprise found your broadcasts to be of immense interest and informative knowledge, not only to a particular religious community, but also to the humanity as a whole. As a Hindu, I enjoy all your programmes with a broad enthusiasm, and think of them as contributory in nature, towards the refinement of soul.'

It is sometimes suggested that secular programmes are like bait concealing an evangelistic hook. It's not a very appealing picture in spite of Christ's promise that his followers (who in fact used nets not hooks) would become 'fishers of men'. It may even remind some readers of the bribes of sweets and cheap gifts used to attract children by some evangelists and Sunday schools.

But there is an important difference between good secular programmes and sweets. It is obvious in the case of news bulletins. The Bible clearly shows that God is concerned not only to save men's souls but to offer them a full life. Whereas hooks harm fish, good secular programmes are not bait, but food to nourish the consumers — 'hooks' made of worms, in fact! Christians are to be salt in society besides 'fishers of men'. As the Ecuador captain realised, a reliable news service is a rare blessing that cannot be taken for granted. Indeed, in the west it is clearly what has been called 'the fruit of the fruit of the Spirit', that is to say, it comes as a result of the influence upon western culture of the Bible and the saving work of the Holy Spirit. God is concerned about truth. Where apostate Christianity or a godless ideology dominates society, truth is bound to suffer. Thus good secular programmes may be seen as a gift that Christianity can offer men just as missionaries have for many years served mankind in the sphere of medicine, education and farming. The Delhi office of FEBA has in fact produced a series of health education programmes which help to meet an immense need in the Indian subcontinent (and in the Third World generally). In addition, it is natural to assume that a source which is trustworthy in speaking of material facts may be relied upon to tell the truth about spiritual matters.

Listening to these health education programmes, however, raises a controversial issue. For they do not limit themselves to health education. It is easy to trace similarities (real or contrived) between the methods used to fight a disease such as cholera and those that the Bible prescribes for healing the universal human 'disease' of sin. This is not very different from the practice, traditional in missionary medicine, of compelling all out-patients to attend a short preaching service before they receive treatment. This tactic, although traditional, has come in for severe criticism and is less common now than it used to be.

The question of principle that it raises is not limited, of course, to health education programmes. RWW's excellent programme for stamp collectors, 'Hobby of Kings', uses a similar method; it tends to include a very obviously Christian item which is certainly linked to the stamps discussed but which cannot by any stretch of the imagination be described as of philatelic interest.

In *Slim Fingers* (Christian Literature Crusade, 1976) Phil Booth tells an interesting story about this programme. It begins with a WEC missionary in India plagued first thing every morning until 7.30 by the blaring transistors of her Indian neighbours. Hopefully she turned on *her* radio and gave the now silent neighbourhood the benefit of FEBA Seychelles. Disappointment — only a programme for stamp-collectors! But either the stamps or the spiritual content interested the Brahmin who stopped by her window, and later asked her which station was broadcasting the programme. When she left to go on furlough, the Brahmin and twenty of his friends were regularly hearing about stamp-collecting and Jesus Christ.

There seems to be no evidence that listeners disapprove of these religious inserts, but they certainly make some 'disinterested', 'service to the community' programmes look far more like old-fashioned 'bait'.

Magazine programmes are arguably in a different category. Here the basic concept is of a series of unrelated items of general interest and although a hard-sell evangelistic approach would clearly be out of place there seems to be no valid argument against including religious material. A good deal depends, of course, on what sort of religious material is used. Thus the

RWW series, 'Books for Banishment', in which people are asked what books they would take into exile with them, obviously derives a Christian colouring from the individuals selected. A magazine programme from a Christian source naturally includes more Christian material than its secular counterparts. But in neither case need there be any hint of preaching, that is of exhorting or even inviting listeners to make some sort of personal commitment.

It is interesting that scarcely any attempt has been made to include direct Christian teaching in the newscasts, although for many years FEBC Manila did include a 30-second Christian comment. The possibilities are obvious. Reference to warfare might be followed by a few words about the Prince of Peace, news of food shortages could lead naturally to a reminder about feeding on the Word of God; the latest murder might suggest Matt. 5:21ff. and the link between anger and murder. If we ask why this method of 'preaching the gospel' has generally been rejected, the answer could be that giving accurate news is recognised as a worthwhile activity in itself (unlike health education?) which does not need to be further justified in terms of evangelism.

The news services of both the BBC and the Voice of America are trusted all over the world by listeners who may be rather sceptical about what they hear on local stations. The results of the 1973 India Survey (described on pages 113ff.) are very clear.

Question 18 was 'Why do you listen to short-wave foreign stations?'

The answer 'for reliable news' was given by 550 of the 1,135 Tamil-speaking respondents; 330 of the 843 who spoke Telegu; 400 of the 782 using English, and 350 of the 670 Hindi speakers.

Question 19 followed this up by asking specifically, 'What station or stations do you listen to for reliable news?' 880 of the Tamils listened to the BBC news from FEBA (400), Ceylon (300) or the BBC (180); of the Telegu speakers, whose English tends not to be fluent, 300 listened to All-India Radio, but more than 500 used FEBA, Ceylon, or the BBC. Of the English language listeners 500 chose the BBC, as did 400 of those who speak Hindi.

It is hard to exaggerate the importance of these findings. They show that a reliable news service is a very strong factor indeed in determining which stations people listen to — and once they are tuned in they are presumably likely to go on listening. It is also clear that people will respect and value a station that offers such a service. Christian broadcasters may well feel themselves privileged to be of use in this way. On one occasion at least, a Christian station 'scooped' a very important story. When the Ethiopian Emperor, Haile Selassie, was deposed in 1974, the first news came from Radio Voice of the Gospel, a Lutheran station in Addis Ababa, and RVOG was given credit for the story in early BBC bulletins, until confirmation came from the agencies.

FEBC (Manila) sees news as so important that it provides a ten-minute bulletin every hour, and includes a number of items relevant to the Philippines. They tactfully devoted a solid five minutes to a book written by the Philippine president.

FEBA Seychelles has made use of the BBC World Service bulletins. (British readers interested in sampling these may hear them at various times of the day and night on either 1088 or 1295 KHz.) They are infinitely better than those presented for home consumption, since they focus on events of real importance and give little coverage to the activities of criminals, pop stars and publicity seekers. All the same, they are naturally slanted towards British news and this makes them less than ideal for the listeners FEBA aims to reach. These would prefer to have the BBC's excellent coverage of world news supplemented with stories about India and other places 'east of Suez'.

Establishing a news service sounds straightforward but calls for a well-thought-out policy, the right equipment and the right staff. The last two cost money! So far as equipment is concerned the problem is purely financial. It is a question of paying for the installation of 'ticker-tape' machines which stand in a room and spew forth miles of printed tape, carrying minute by minute details of events all over the world. This news is provided by a press agency such as Associated Press (AP) and Reuters. The agencies are able to make a living and employ staff because clients all over the world pay for the service they supply.

But what happens to the stacks of teleprinter tape? Somebody has to select material from this and edit it into a bulletin lasting five, ten or fifteen minutes. To 'edit' means to rewrite, abbreviating drastically and picking out the most important points from a mass of detail. The task is made more difficult because fresh information is constantly coming in: imagine, for example, the variety of stories engendered by a revolution in progress — even while a bulletin is being broadcast, news may be received of a new flare-up, a set-back for one side, or a ceasefire.

Expertise is also needed in the selection and editing of the less important stories. The really big items choose themselves, but it needs skill to see which of the hundreds of other ones to choose and how to present them in a way that will grip the wandering interest of the audience. A further complication occurs when the news service is beamed into different regions and in different languages. The Swahili service for Africa would be bound to include different items from those in an English language service for India, and even those required for both might call for skilful translation (what's the Swahili for 'floating' currency?).

At the time of writing, a news room, two teleprinters and other equipment are available on Mahé. Ken Stewart, who is now responsible for the news service, has had wide experience in journalism and radio. At various times he has been Features Editor of a Malayan daily paper, deputy chief of Reuter's Fleet Street Africa desk, and Chief News Editor of RVOG in Ethiopia. Other members of the team are his wife Sally who also has experience in radio and journalism and Alan and

Sheila Hyman (Alan formerly worked for BBC local and national news services).

The September 1976 schedule at the end of this book (p.155f.) shows the programmes transmitted in English from Mahé. (For most listeners, the time would be four or five hours later than GMT.) Thursday's programmes are typical of the strategy adopted. During the morning the religious content is limited, (although not absent) until 'Radio Today' which features Dr John Nederhood of the Canadian Christian Reformed Church, and which offers Christian teaching, solidly biblical but realistic, interesting and topical. At first hearing this might seem to be useful only to committed Christians who want to learn more of their faith and its practical implications. But in fact a seriously interested non-Christian would likely find the series uniquely helpful as a means of gaining insight into Christianity. This is because the 'Radio Today' programme (heard elsewhere as 'Back to God'), unlike some devoted to simple biblical exposition, is careful to apply biblical truth to human interests and problems.

There is a pattern in the placing of these programmes. The general principle is to move from what the uncommitted listener wants to hear to what the programmer most wants to be heard.

The same pattern can be seen in the later transmissions. 'Radio Newsreel' is a current affairs programme from the BBC World Service. 'Roundabout' is a magazine programme. 'Hidden Treasures' offers a complete contrast. It is the first and at the time of writing the only English language Bible teaching programme made in India by an Indian national for FEBC/FEBA and is transmitted from the Seychelles and Manila. Zac Poonen, who records it in Bangalore, is well known as a Bible teacher and writer. Here is one listener's testimony to what is intended simply as a Bible teaching series:

'Your radio message brought me to real light and by that my life is meaningful now. Realising my weakness and the impossibilities of overcoming it, several times I thought of committing suicide. But one day as I passed through a small house in the night I happened to hear someone preaching but it was from the radio. I made enquiry about the time and meter band and I listened daily, it changed me completely and now I have the peace and I am happy. Please pray for my victorious Christian life.'

'Back to the Bible', which ends the day from Monday to Friday, offers straight Bible exposition, featuring the veteran Bible teacher, Theodore Epp.

CHAPTER 7

Looking for Trouble?

FROM ONE POINT of view, FEBA may be seen as largely a 'service' organisation enabling programme suppliers to speak to the people they are trying to reach.

Some of these programme suppliers are individuals, evangelists or preachers who use radio to extend their ministry. Others are based on a local church, or supported by a denomination, or by a missionary society. It is important for understanding Christian radio to be clear about this: that most programmes transmitted do not originate with the transmitting station, but with a 'programme supplier' who approaches the station in order to ensure that a radio audience actually hears the tapes that have been recorded.

At first sight it may seem that these programme suppliers should bear sole responsibility for the programmes broadcast in their names. In fact, the situation is rather complex.

Imagine (and this is only an imaginary case) three programme suppliers each supplying a 15-minute programme broadcast in the same language, one after the other. The content of programme A is excellent, but unfortunately it is badly recorded and so many listeners have switched off after five minutes that scarcely anybody listens to programmes B and C. In the words of Lord Reith, the first Director General of the BBC, 'Radio gives the greatest number of people the quickest exit.' Programme B, by contrast, is beautifully recorded. Unfortunately it consists of a 15-minute sermon by an elderly preacher who devotes all his time to expounding his own views about a minute but controversial point connected with the Second Coming. A few enthusiasts listen with great interest, but many other potential listeners are bored, and some are upset to hear their own biblically based beliefs attacked. Programme C, on the other hand, is excellent and makes good use of some very attractive music. Too late this is recognised as coming from a pornographic revue that has been delighting and scandalising London and New York.

'Imaginary', we said, but unfortunately these examples are founded on fact. They show clearly why FEBA must exercise some control over the programmes they broadcast. This need to behave responsibly towards listeners, suppliers, and the thousands of Christians who have given money so that the work may go on is sufficiently important to be looked at in some detail. What does programme monitoring involve?

'Station Regulations and Guidelines for Programme Suppliers' have been drawn up for guidance. First of all, every programme must be in sympathy with the FEBA doctrinal basis. The only exception is 'general interest' programmes, which contain little religious material, and even these may be edited if they contain material contrary to FEBA policy.

Secondly, doctrinal arguments and controversy about topics outside the FEBA basis must be avoided. The importance of this is clear, but it's not always easy to decide what is controversial. *This* programme supplier, for example, may feel that another programme referring frequently to spiritual healing is highly controversial, while the supplier of *that* programme sees spiritual healing as a simple and basic element in telling the Good News.

Third, a positive attitude must be maintained. There should be no negative attacks against people or organisations, whether political or religious. Objective evaluation in the light of plain biblical teaching is another matter. One programme supplier was surprised to find he was not allowed to use FEBA facilities to mount a vigorous attack on Communism.

Fourth, music must be selected in accordance with these

criteria, and with the cultural tastes of the target audience. In general, certain types of 'secular' music must be avoided: vocal music with immoral or suggestive lyrics; instrumental arrangements of such songs; theme music from films known for their immoral stories; music performed by musicians notoriously anti-Christian or immoral.

Obviously it is not easy to apply these standards consistently, but it is equally obvious that some such effort must be made. People often feel quite strongly about music. Christians tend to approve of 'sacred' music such as they are used to hearing in whatever church they attend. They may also disapprove bitterly of what they regard as 'wordly' music, a tendency shown in the way one Christian station (not FEBA) treated a late-night Christian 'pop' programme. Although permitted to use the transmitter, the programme was effectively isolated from more conventional material. The English-speaking announcer simply said goodnight 'at the end of the day's broadcasting' after which a programme in Arabic was transmitted before the suspect programme (a first-rate English language one!) was allowed to take the air.

Music also divides Indian Christians. Many congregations who worship in English are accustomed to western church music. But the use of western music is bound to brand Christianity as alien. In fact, the music preferred by many Indians is a blend of Indian classical music and western 'pop', heard incessantly on Radio Ceylon and used in the Hindi films which are so important a part of Indian popular culture today. It makes good sense to use this 'film music' style for Christian programmes and the Tamil 'Voice of Love' programme (made at the Hindustan Bible Institute in Madras) does so to great effect, utilising professional Indian musicians who give their services free. A listener's letter shows how greatly Indian music is appreciated. 'What a privilege it is to hear lovely messages and tear-compelling songs. May I suggest that some of the most moving melodies, which are quite new to many people, often go unrelished and ungrasped. I am sure it is all the more difficult to make it any more clear, audible and articulate. My point is Indian vernacular programmes are deeply appreciated by all listeners, but English melodies are a bit difficult to follow.'

But many Indian *Christians* (whose attitude to the cinema is in any case very much the same as was taken by Anglo-Saxon evangelicals in the thirties), disapprove of this and regard it as dangerous compromise. Obviously the chief concern should be what the guidelines refer to as 'the culture tastes of the target audience' but it calls for a good deal of Holy-Spirit-given determination to keep this in mind when fellow-believers are prophesying woe, denouncing worldliness and even threatening to withdraw support.

There are still more factors to be considered before a programme, or more precisely a series of programmes, can be accepted for transmission. Clearly the technical quality must be adequate. If *one* of several programmes in (say) Tamil is difficult to listen to then *other* programmes in the same language will attract a smaller audience since people will have switched off in despair or found another station. For the same reason, it is vital not to bore listeners. Many broadcasters who are accustomed to preaching to big congregations tend to speak in a way which, while it might be appropriate in a large church, is quite out of place at the microphone. Listeners who enjoy being spoken to in their homes may dislike being preached at. So FEBA reserves the right to edit or reject programmes which are 'deemed inappropriate for international Christian broadcasting' whether in respect of 'content or technical quality'. It is also necessary to provide programmes in multiples of thirteen — three months at a time.

In the light of all that has been said, it will be clear that monitoring programmes is a difficult as well as a responsible job. Somebody has to listen to and evaluate every tape sent to Bangalore for use on Mahé.

It is not surprising that two Indian workers who spend much of their time in this way, say the job is demanding but sometimes rather boring. They are very conscious of the difficulty (even with help from other people) of keeping tabs on programmes in eighteen languages including Tibetan. Their knowledge of film music (especially films 'known for their immoral stories') is limited. They realise that new suppliers may need guidance about technique or content. They recognise on the other hand that some suppliers have difficulty in supplying first-rate tapes because their equipment is poor. They have become painfully aware of the repetitive nature of many programmes; 'Song, message, song — and you must put the gospel across, all in a quarter of an hour.' This sort of programme is sometimes known as a 'hymn sandwich'. It's not surprising one of the workers should welcome the opportunity to get involved with people in pastoral and youth work. Yet even after hearing thousands of programmes and evaluating them on the inevitable pro formas they still look forward to hearing such programmes as 'Youth takes the Air' and 'It's Your World'. They believe one of the greatest needs is for programmes that relate Christianity to everyday issues rather than generalised preaching.

Inevitably there is sometimes friction between suppliers and monitoring service. One supplier spoke witheringly of an adverse comment passed back on one section of a programme — 'The speaker is very fast and emotional!' So he was; he had been telling the story of a fire with people shouting for help — a good illustration that was (apparently) not fully understood by the person who monitored the tape and who, not being fluent in the language used, may have responded to the tone rather than the words. But this (friendly) critic of the system did not for a moment suggest that programme monitoring should cease; in fact he saw a need for it to be done more thoroughly and consistently.

It is pointless to take trouble to monitor the quality of the programmes transmitted if listeners find difficulty in receiving them. Phil Booth is pointing to a serious problem of Christian radio when he suggests that 'if the listener needs an above-average receiver or a high degree of loyalty to the Christian cause in order to be able to listen to programmes, it is doubtful if we are really doing our job' (*Ears that Hear*, RWW, London 1966, p. 7).

Transmitter engineers can use their knowledge of power, aerial design and prevalent conditions to estimate what sort of signal listeners are likely to get in a given area. But nothing can take the place of first-hand listening experience. How can broadcasters find out what reception is really like? Listeners' letters provide some information but this is bound to be patchy and subjective. What A regards as 'fair', B will call 'poor'. (B may in any case have a better receiver.)

A more useful source of information are letters and cards from DX-ers giving precise details of date, time, and frequency together with a more objective analysis of reception quality. Many stations gratefully acknowledge such reports and in return issue QSL cards which are collected by DX-ers.

Nothing is so helpful as regular reports from professional or semi-professional 'monitors' who listen regularly and submit what are called SINFO reports. These initials stand for: **S**ignal strength; **I**nterference (from other stations); **N**oise (i.e. atmospheric); **F**ading; **O**verall quality. Each is assessed on a five-point scale so that SINFO 55555 would imply perfection whereas SINFO 42222 would lead the transmitter engineers to consider using another frequency or transmitting at a different time.

Every missionary radio station depends on reports from monitors, many of whom expect no payment for the hours of regular listening which are needed if their reports are to be of value. The need is especially great when a transmitter first comes into use, when frequencies are changed or when a new reception area is aimed at. But the continuous changes in atmospheric conditions, solar activity and transmissions from other sources mean that this unspectacular service is always needed.

CHAPTER 8

'Respectable Aunty'

THE SERVICE IS over, and the preacher takes his place by the door. 'Thank you for that message — it *was* a help!' 'You know, I'd often wondered about that verse you explained; I can understand it now.' 'I was very surprised to hear that you approve of —. I don't see how a Christian could get involved in *that.*' And, more occasionally, 'If you could spare the time during the week there's something I'd like to ask you about.'

It's all so normal, so much part of the life of a preacher — until he exchanges the church for a studio and directs his words towards a microphone, not a visible congregation. In doing this the preacher cuts himself off from the people he is serving. He cannot see when their attention wanders or when part of his address sparks their interest. He can hear neither the shifting fidgeting sounds of a bored congregation, nor the encouraging hush as hundreds of listeners concentrate on the words of one man. After he has finished he has no way of following up what he has said — and neither has his audience.

This remoteness from the people being ministered to is a difficulty peculiar to Christians working through radio.[1] Happily the problem is not entirely insoluble.

All the world over, listeners write to radio stations. The BBC External Service, for example, received 350,000 letters in

1. It might, of course, be reduced if more use were made of small local stations, especially in the big cities. But there are good reasons for using fewer and more powerful transmitters, serving a wide area (see p. 126f.).

1974, according to a letter in the *Observer* for November 2, 1975. (BBC World Service is far from being the only agency which even builds a programme out of these listeners' letters.) In just the same way, those who listen to Christian radio programmes can get in touch with speakers by post. And they do so in large numbers. During 1975 FEBAI and programme suppliers working with it received 50,000 letters from listeners in the Indian subcontinent (in the first six months of 1976 the total was 36,000 with the October tally shooting up to 7,600). This is a sizeable mail-bag, but not particularly big by Christian radio standards; 'Back to the Bible' gets 3,000 per day at its Lincoln, Nebraska, headquarters.

Programmes vary greatly in their capacity to draw a response. A survey by HCJB, Quito, found that two 15-minute programmes (from Radio Worldwide) drew a 90 per cent greater response than any other half-hour of English language broadcasting.

Why do people write? Leoda Buckwalter, wife of the Director of FEBAI, suggests seven reasons: (1) Because of interest created by listening to the programmes, especially if they have personal need of any kind. (2) Because the programme suppliers are anonymous and people feel they can share their problems with them. (3) Because in India a great deal of emphasis is put upon the prayers and blessings of those who are considered 'holy men', in this case, men and women of God. (4) Because of genuine spiritual hunger and thirst created by the Holy Spirit as the listener hears a clear presentation of Jesus Christ over the air. (5) Some seek more material benefits — jobs, or security or the glamour of sponsorship abroad. (6) Prayer partners write in to send their donations and to pledge their prayer sponsorship for the work. (7) Prayer partners also share on a spiritual level — both victories and prayer requests.

Very few responses are hostile, but quite often listeners request extended time or a changed time for programmes they value. Music programmes attract a wide response, and programmes in English elicit letters from all over India but especially from areas such as Tamil Nadu or Assam with a heavy concentration of Christians. Requests for Scripture portions, literature and Bible study courses are always welcomed.

Some listeners write simply to share their pleasure in listening to the programmes: 'Accept my deep appreciation of the well planned programmes to which I listen daily. It is like the dripping of honey from the honey comb. As I listen to the talks I seem to hear Jesus and my heart is thrilled with deep joy.' Such letters are a great encouragement to everybody connected with a programme. They may also be very useful since they often throw light on the circumstances in which people listen, as in this letter from a Muslim country: 'While I was sitting down studying for my exams I turned on my dial and your voice came on by accident. Then I closed the book and listened to the end. Since this time I have become fond of your programmes and I wait for it with much interest. Please send me a portion of the Bible. Thanks.'

Whereas in the west a radio will be used by an individual or family, in less developed nations it may attract a larger audience: 'I listen to your programmes every Saturday. Even though this programme is done primarily for children, everyone benefits from it . . . the older folk, the young people and the children. Why? Because you present the things of God. Yes, you children's story-teller, your manner is very beautiful. May God bless this programme even more. Members of 6 families gather to listen.' What an incentive for the broadcaster!

Another letter from a Muslim country shows a whole family becoming involved through the interest of one member: 'Your letter has brought joy and happiness to my heart. I read your book to my parents. They listened to all what was read admiring what they have been hearing. At last my father took over and he began to read for us and to explain it to us.'

A theme that recurs again and again is the isolation of many listeners. The radio may be their only source of Christian fellowship; even when there is a local church it may be small and struggling. Such is the case of this listener from East Africa: 'I have enjoyed listening to many of your programmes this past year. Often I thought of writing, but failed to put the thought into action. I doubt if you get many letters from this land. I appreciated the messages you brought from the Keswick Convention several months ago. The number of Christians here is not large and in the absence of the larger Christian fellowship, I do enjoy the Bible teaching and the good music you give.'

Similar letters come from India: 'We are living in agency area where we do not have churches and preachers, we depend upon the radio messages as our church. These messages are helping us. Please show us the Way of Salvation through your prayers.'

'We are the only two Christian families amongst 1,400 people in our village; we listen to the words of God through the radio as our Church programme. Praise the Lord we are getting spiritual message to the glory of God. Really your programmes are spiritually useful to us. May the Lord help you to give more of these messages to the Marathi people through your ministry.'

'All the members of my family are receiving spiritual benefits from your programmes. There are very few Christian people around here. There are no churches, the nearest one is twenty miles away. One receives spiritual peace through listening to the Christian radio programmes, mornings and evenings. Your programmes are truly heart touching. May God grant you grace, strength and wisdom so that you may continue to produce such programmes. Millions of people are receiving spiritual benefit from them. We tell other people who have radios to listen to these programmes, that they might also derive spiritual benefit.'

It is natural for Christians in the west to see the importance of Christian radio chiefly in terms of its possibilities as a means of evangelising. But the best possible method of spreading good news about Jesus is for Christians to share with their neighbours. When the church is renewed and revived, there is no need to hold conferences about evangelism because it is happening all the time. Certainly if Christian radio could play a part in revitalising the church in India, the results would be incalculable. The letters quoted show how this could happen.

Some of the most isolated listeners are probably those serving in the armed forces. This corporal may come from a Christian home: 'I am in the Indian Air Force and I wish to tell you how deeply I appreciate the radio messages you broadcast — particularly "Jesus Saves". I am far away from my home and I truly am happy to hear the messages whenever it is possible for me to do so.'

The soldier who wrote the following letter apparently turned to Christ as a result of listening to the programmes: 'Your messages through radio are fine. Many have changed their lives by hearing them. I am one of such sepoys. Pray for me and my repented life so that I walk strongly in the Lord.'

Perhaps the most eloquent of all are the words of a soldier on the border guard who feels himself challenged by what he has heard: 'I do praise the Lord for help from the programmes for sinners like me. I was grateful for the message on Abraham when you spoke of his belief and obedience. I pray that until the time of God's second coming, He will give you strength, knowledge, wisdom to teach His holy words. I praise the Lord for His love and protection. I am listening to your pastor regularly. I am a great criminal — God has given me a task of killing. Like the seed falling among thorn bushes and the good seed being choked, I am a wicked man. I am an army border guard whose duty is to kill. I am 20 years. My home is in KK Dist. and now I am in the snows of the Himalayas . . . Please help me.'

Perhaps the writer of the following was not completely isolated — apparently there was a church for him to attend. But although not a few men have been converted in such circumstances, jails are not noted for plentiful Christian fellowship: 'I am well by God's grace. I am very grateful for the literature sent me. I listen every week to your messages. I go regularly to the church in jail and invite friends to go with me. Mk.2:17. I pray as the Lord's child Ps.34:8. After reading literature I distributed it to friends. Send more if you can . . .'

Sometimes a programme or feature is mentioned, and this helps to reassure those responsible that they are providing what some people at least want to hear. This student, for example, obviously appreciates some of the 'secular' content: 'Being a student of physics and very interested in popularising that subject, I am glad that you've included the programme "Focus on Physics" presented by Radio Worldwide.'

Here is an appreciation of the value of a Telegu programme designed to help local churches by improving the quality of Sunday School teaching: 'We have a Sunday School but we do not know how to teach them properly. Now we are learning by listening to Subodhana Sarani radio programme. We have fifteen juniors and twenty sub-junior, that is, primary children. We are four teachers here and please send us Sunday School books, pictures and flannel graph pictures. Please send them and we will teach accordingly.'

The regular music programme from the Seychelles obviously appeals to some listeners: 'For the past couple of days I am very much interested in your programmes that were broadcast during the morning session of your station from 11.30 a.m. The first half hour instrumental music is really a good starter by any day.'

But religious music is also popular — and effective: 'The other day I accidentally listened to your broadcast. It has changed my life. The devotional songs which were broadcast played a predominant role in my life as a turning point. The lyrics and hymns which are full of meaning. I had never realised before, though I have been singing in the church. It gives me so much of comfort and bliss.'

From a Muslim country comes an interesting and encouraging response to an attempt to adapt Christianity to a non-western culture. The Koran, the sacred book of Islam, is often chanted by Muslims, rather than read. What could be more appropriate than to do the same with the Christian holy book the Bible? It obviously appealed to this listener, and presumably to others: 'I am a 16-year-old girl and I listen to the beautiful chanting of the Gospel. When one listens to these chantings he cannot help but write you thanking the Brother who chants. Please send me his records.'

Most encouraging of all, of course, are the many letters from listeners who have turned to Christ because of what they have heard. This man's experience will be familiar to fellow-believers all over the world: 'I was a man who never believed in any gods. Though I have heard much about Christians' God it made no impression on me. Recently I happened to hear your radio programmes in Malayalam and it influenced me and enabled me to think of my life, life after death. I began to read the Bible for my problems as someone suggested. The more I studied God spoke to me much and it gave me a new life and peace. The Bible answered and solved all my questions and problems. I request you to pray for me. I am extremely happy to inform you that what you have aimed in your programmes is fulfilled in my life.'

The following letter from North Africa is expressed in less familiar language. Readers who know something of Islam may recognise some characteristic turns of phrase. But the experience is no less typical: 'Sincere greetings from the bottom of my heart which is filled with love and loyalty to this voice, the voice of the Holy Spirit. I am writing you this letter after I have been saturated with this spiritual religion, Christianity, through your literature. Your publications have thrilled my inner being and prompted me to write you about what goes through my mind of spiritual matters. The voice of Christ kept ringing in my mind and coming to me wherever I went and in whatever I did. Truly Christ is great. He came to this world to save us by His Spirit in order that we might live peaceably. He also died for our sakes and in order to exalt the Word of the Most High. How ignorant we were in that we did not go all the way in serving Him. How ignorant we were in that we did not walk in His redeeming way wherein lies our peace and rest. This pure religion, Christianity, leads us to eternal life, the life of graciousness and respectability. This voice, Dear Brother, kept ringing in my ears and inner being, saying, "I am your Saviour, the Forgiver of your sins, O ignorant and ungrateful man." Man fell in sin since the days of Adam and will continue in it till the end. But God sent Christ to give us forgiveness. The Lord Jesus Christ accepted me when I confessed my sins to Him.'

Letters such as these call for something more than a formal answer, and make considerable demands on the workers who deal with correspondence. Often, of course, they have other responsibilities as well. Large organisations can allocate staff exclusively to this task, but smaller programme suppliers expect workers to accept a number of different roles. Wives often help with this work; producers likewise. (Technical specialists are usually fully occupied with their specialised responsibilities.)

Obviously, some individuals are better at 'follow-up' than others, and every station or programme supplier will have people who specialise or semi-specialise in this ministry. So why (the reader may ask) should FEBA not provide a team to be responsible for follow-up work covering all programmes transmitted? Then at the end of every broadcast, the invitation would be the same — to write to FEBA, Mahé, Seychelles.

There are several reasons for not doing this. (1) The cost of providing such a service (postage, maintenance for the staff) would increase the expense to programme suppliers of transmitting from Seychelles. In other words, air time would cost more. (2) It is far more encouraging and also cheaper for the listener to be invited to write to an address in his own country than to somewhere remote — a place he may not even have heard of. (3) Answering listeners' letters requires (as we shall see) knowledge of the social and religious background. Obviously the people best qualified are those who live and work in the culture from which the letters come. (4) This is especially true of language. A Gujarati or Malayalam speaker who has heard a programme in his own language will most likely write — and expect a reply — in that language. (5) If the programme suppliers receive and answer listeners' letters they will be made aware day by day of the sort of response they are getting. They will, hopefully, be able to praise God for success and pray about problems. This is infinitely better than simply providing programmes without any knowledge of their effectiveness.

Some of the most interesting and encouraging letters come from non-Christians who have been challenged by what they have heard. Perhaps they are clearly experiencing what some would call a sense of conviction and need. 'I am a Hindu boy. One day suddenly I heard on 31 meters in my radio, your programme. When I heard message of the crucifixion of Lord Jesus I felt I am crying, thank you for the message you broadcasted. Now my heart is eager to learn about Jesus Christ. Please send me some literature.'

Another writes: 'I want to receive Lord Jesus Christ as my personal saviour. Please send me some books to lead me to Christ. Please also send me Bible lessons.'

Often the correspondent feels strongly attracted by Christianity or, more precisely, by Jesus Christ: 'Every day I listen to the Christian programmes regularly. It brings great peace to my heart and I am very much influenced and attracted towards Christ.' Another example: 'Even though I am Hindu when I hear your programmes I am able to understand the life of Christ and am filled with joy. Please increase time of broadcast.'

A letter may represent the result of months or years of thoughtful and earnest seeking for truth: 'I listen to your programmes every day in the morning and in the evening. The programmes are very excellent to the best of my knowledge. Jesus is the only messenger of God who can forget the sins of people as like me. I want to get under Jesus Christ. I am Hindu by religion and by caste a Brahmin. There are so many evils in my religion and so I want to accept Jesus Christ as a religious leader. I want to know more about Jesus Christ and His life. So please send a few books about Jesus Christ forthwith. I am also a student of so many Bible Correspondence Institutes which tells about the life of Christ. I have got knowledge and now I am in a condition to say that Jesus is the only God who can save us from our sins. Now I am totally satisfied with Jesus and there is no doubt present at this time; however, I also want to get further knowledge about Jesus. So please send me the books which are necessary for a person who is seeking to know about Jesus Christ. Let me also know where I should apply to change my religion, please note that this is very important.'

The writer of the letter quoted above has apparently come to a definite decision. Sometimes a response which is similarly warm and positive may be difficult to evaluate. Has the Muslim who wrote this letter already become a Christian, or is he simply attracted by Jesus? 'May God greet you with a sincere greeting. Your voice comes in strongly and clearly these days in spite of the thunder storms and the heavy rains we are having. Your broadcasts are different from others in that you have a great figure or emblem namely the Teacher and Leader, the Holy Christ whose name God exalted and preserved in the highest heavens. This broadcast does not side with master or slaves or certain groups of people but rather it exalts the Man who fought for the happiness of the human race. He exhorted the people to worship God only. I hear on your broadcasts these days, many talks about the life of Christ. You also promise literature to listeners and send them the Bible without charge. Therefore, I am asking you to send me by return mail the Holy Book and an account of the blessed immortal life of Christ. Many thanks for all the excellent services that you offer in order that the listeners might know the realities of the Man Teacher, the Christ.'

Another Muslim correspondent who, like the man quoted above, listens to ELWA programmes, realises that approving of Jesus Christ is not the same as trusting him: 'I listen daily to your broadcast from ELWA in Monrovia, Liberia, although of course I do not believe in all of what the station says. There is a great difference between what I have learned and inherited from my fathers and forefathers and what ELWA teaches. But in spite of that something within me keeps drawing me to tune in to the Voice of Pardon (ELWA). One day while I was playing with my radio dial I came across a sister station TWR, and I began listening to these two stations regularly. I was able to get quite a bit of literature on Jesus Christ. And I enjoyed it. *But there is a great difference between admiration and faith.* I have talked with you frankly and I wish to get more literature. Many thanks.'

Many factors combine to influence us in any decision we may make — spiritual or 'secular'. Listeners do not live in a vacuum and radio programmes are often only one factor in spiritual development, as the following makes clear: 'I am writing to you by the persuasion of my friend . . . He has told me about having a personal relationship with Jesus. At first, I drew back because my family are orthodox Hindus and believe firmly in the Hindu religion. But I've been reading about Jesus and my understanding is opening. By learning to know about Him and seeing His great mercy, I have been greatly influenced. I want salvation from my sins and I want to serve the Lord. Please advise me and help me.'

The letter just quoted shows how Christians may use radio programmes to back up their own attempts to tell others about Jesus. But many listeners feel they have nobody close at hand who can answer their questions: 'I was taken back for a minute by hearing parts of "Who is a Christian?" I am enclosing Rs.1 as I want to read that book. Can you answer some questions as I have some doubts: What is meant by the will of God (Matt.7:21); What is meant by treasures in heaven (Matt. 6:20)?'

The extracts printed above show clearly what a great responsibility rests upon the Christian workers who answer these letters. There are so many requests for advice or literature and responding to them is not always easy. The follow-up worker must have the gift — or skill — of sympathetic insight into the correspondent's needs and the ability to 'read between the lines'. A varied stock of literature is important, and the worker must be familiar with its contents, in order to select what will be most helpful.

The letters already quoted show how often listeners request a copy of the Bible or other Christian literature. 'With due respect and humble submission, I beg to state that I heard your programme of spetual power in Radio on short wave. I am very intrust in this programme for family. I want to know your next time programme in detail and request for Bible book in Punjabi or Urdu or English in three any language. I shall be highly thankful to you on this act of kindness.'

What could be more appealing than the following, from a young man living in a government student hostel? 'I want to know about Jesus Christ. I desire a new testament as I want to study it before I go to sleep at night.'

It is very common for programme suppliers to offer a portion of the Bible or a copy of the 'message' spoken to any correspondent who asks for them. To (relatively) affluent westerners this may seem barely worth mentioning. But in a Third World setting, where people own very little indeed, a copy of the Bible, or of any book at all, is a valued possession, and any 'free gift' offer is likely to boost the number of letters received. (Where a programme supplier quotes one or two months' figures only for letters received it may be as well for anyone interested in gaining an accurate picture of what has happened to check whether the increase in letters received is due to the station's programmes' growing popularity or to a free gift offer.)

Some correspondents try to use the programme supplier as a potential source of financial or material help. This may surprise people who know that missionary radio workers are usually not at all affluent by western standards. But it is the most natural thing imaginable, if one takes into account the appalling poverty of the Third World. By such standards the radio workers are very wealthy. Surely (the writer thinks) they can spare something, or 'pull strings' to help the needy? Sometimes the requests are direct and straightforward. Sometimes they are more oblique. It is, after all, not unknown in the west to ask for 'prayer' when seeking money!

'I am very happy over the radio messages broadcasting from Seychelles. I have accepted Lord Jesus Christ as my personal Saviour. I have seen God's Vision that I would buy a tractor. So we thought that we would buy under self-employment scheme. God has provided everything we needed by His grace. We have to pay 10 per cent of the amount. When another person promised us to pay this amount and he did not then the whole plan is upset. We don't know why it is happened. Why God cannot do this. We want build a prayer hall in my village. Please pray for these two points in your prayer.'

Requests for help in gaining education, or a job either in India or overseas, are not uncommon. It is less usual to be asked for help in publishing a manuscript. 'I received your letter and two books along with it. The children in my house listen regularly to the FEBA programmes. We have established a FEBA listeners' radio club. Old and young, everybody listens to your programme with great interest and all of them have believed in the Lord Jesus Christ. One of the children has started asking for literature in my name. Kindly continue to send literature and books related to Jesus Christ and the Holy Bible. We have been taking the Voice of Prophecy Bible correspondence course from Poona and have passed exams but they haven't returned the certificate yet. I have composed some poems relating to Jesus Christ but they haven't been published yet. However, two or three of them have been broadcast from RVOG in Addis Ababa. I hope you will help me financially to print them.'

Perhaps the most remarkable request came from a prisoner in a (European) jail who wanted help in finding a wife!

We have already seen that the tendency to ask for gifts is to be understood against the background of cultures very different from that of the west. It is also obvious that the phrases used in a letter need to be understood in the light of the writer's cultural background. Thus, for a Hindu to describe Jesus as 'Saviour of the world' need by no means imply any change of faith. 'Quaint' English, which might in the UK or USA suggest that the writer is poorly educated, holds no such implication when it comes from a correspondent for whom English is a second language. How many readers of this book would even attempt to write a letter in German or Russian?

'Respectable Aunty, I heard that you will send a free copy of Bible for the have not. I belong to Hindu religion, I doesn't have a Bible, so please send me the Holy Bible.'

Letters such as the following are a reminder that even baptism and the taking of a 'Christian' name may have implications unfamiliar to the western mind: 'I have kept faith newly in the Lord Jesus. I have understood His love. I want to know more about Him. I request you to send me the history books on Jesus. My original name was Siddamallu but my second name after baptism is Yesupadam' (the foot of Jesus).

And the not uncommon request in the next letter must be understood in the light of the universal Hindu practice (not unknown, after all, in Christian circles!) of using pictures of the god worshipped. The writer is not expecting to get a press agency photograph. 'I heard your programme this morning about the Lord Jesus Christ. The things I heard made my heart very warm and brought a change into our thinking. But since I am ignorant about this, please write and instruct me, and please send a picture of Jesus Christ.'

The plea, 'please write and instruct me', is familiar to readers of the Acts. An Ethiopian who had been reading his Bible (the Old Testament, to be precise) made a similar request to Philip. 'Do you understand what you are reading?' 'How can I, unless some one guides me?' (Acts 8:30, 31.) A worker heavily involved in correspondence comments: 'We are

"Philips" in the desert with the "eunuchs" to open the Word to needy hearts.'

Sometimes, of course, the request is made directly, not by letter. An Operation Mobilisation worker tells how 'a friend was walking through a village and heard a Christian programme coming over someone's radio. He went to where the sound was coming from and found an illiterate farmer listening to FEBA Seychelles. He asked him (Philip-like) whether he understood what he was hearing, to which the reply was "No, but I'd like to." My friend was able to lead him to Christ on the spot.'

Even a listener coming from a Christian culture may well want further explanation of points touched upon in a broadcast. How much more if his background is non-Christian! A Muslim writes from Bangladesh: 'Warm greetings to you in the name of Allah. As your pen request, I am writing and hope the correspond between us will continue. I have a question — what is sin? Which is the greatest sin? I hope you will send me some more Christian books and literature.'

A Telegu-speaking Hindu is less restricted in the range of his questions: 'Please tell me why Jesus was born into this world. You spoke about Noah — who is this man? Who has written the Bible? In which language was it first written? Why are you spending so much time for radio broadcasting? What do you get by doing this? Please let me know all about my doubts and clear from them.'

A college student raises the most basic issue of all in a forthright no-nonsense manner: 'Here I want to clear off my doubt. That is the Hindu preaches that God is one, i.e. Sri Vishnu. Muslim Koran says that Mohammed is the only God.[2] You Christians say that Jesus is the only God. If it is the case in what way your Christianity is superior to other religions? I hope that you will certainly clear my doubt in a reasonable manner giving answer to my doubt.'

And as soon as a listener begins to read the Bible for himself

2. It is not only Christians who misunderstand the beliefs of others!

it is only to be expected that all sorts of questions present themselves: 'I listen regularly and it has removed doubts and given much help. Now I look for further help. In Gen.2:17 there is a warning that disobedience would bring death; yet in Gen.5:5 Adam lived 930 years. Is it that this refers to spiritual death? Show me the verses. In Gen.1:3 God created light, but in verses 14–18 He created day and night, the sun. Please explain this that there was light before the sun and moon were created. Also in Romans 5:15 we see that before the law there was no sin. If that is true why did God destroy the world in Noah's day? Please explain . . .'

As we have seen, it is policy, for FEBA at least, that those who provide a programme should be responsible also for correspondence and follow-up. But it is doubtful whether all programme suppliers are competent to deal with complex philosophical and doctrinal questions. And although some control is exercised over the doctrinal and technical quality of the material broadcast, there is no way of making a similar check on what is written.

If it is sometimes difficult to deal with 'intellectual' problems, then it is almost impossible, humanly speaking, to cope with some of the other needs expressed by correspondents. In spite of the 'extended family' system which is characteristic of what we used to call 'backward' peoples, there are still many lonely individuals, and many who have problems which they feel they can't share with anybody. Such listeners are attracted (as they are the whole world over) by the anonymity of the programme suppliers and this in itself encourages them to share their problems.

Another important factor is the third reason mentioned above on p. 90. The writer of this letter, for example, seems to be seeking what some Christians would describe as a 'spiritual director'. 'Can I write and tell you all my troubles? Will you help me, how to find victory over my temptations? Please write and tell me about the spirits of the dead. What happens to them? What do they do, etc. etc.? I shall always write to you for help and counsel and please do help me to be faithful to Jesus my Saviour.'

A Christian girl faces a combination of spiritual depression and family tension: 'I find comfort in your programmes. I am the 18-year-old daughter in a Christian family. I love God. My family are poor but all love God. I am tested very much in this sinful world. I have no rest or happiness. I don't understand why I know so many trials. In all this I will not forget my Saviour. I read, pray, but no comfort. I ask the Lord to think on me His daughter and show me my unknown faults and lead me in straight paths but the Lord does not answer me. Why? The Lord spoke with me during the night. He gave me verses from the Bible. I told my parents but they scolded me saying that I saw Satan and he deceived me. Because of this, my witness that I am His child seems to be false. Pray for me a sinner. Even if God does not answer *my* prayers He will answer yours.'

A woman in extremely difficult circumstances asks simply for prayer: 'I am a Hindu but I believe in the Lord Jesus Christ as the only true God these 23 years in my life, I do have a lot of opposition from both my parents and my husband. I have 3 sons and 1 daughter. On account of my faith my husband has deserted us since 2 years. As in Acts 16:31 will you and all your fellow-workers pray that my children and husband be saved only accept the Lord Jesus Christ as our God?'

Another listener wants to be put in touch with a broadcaster who has inspired confidence: 'I am a regular listener to FEBA programmes and I write to tell you that these talks and music have helped me a great deal in my darkest hours. Gordon Berry's talks have comforted me very much and kept my faith in God alive, when I was sorely tried. I would like to get his advice on a couple of matters, and would like to know if he could help me through private correspondence. Kindly give me his address, so that I could write to him directly. Thanking you and assuring you of my prayers always.'

Sometimes the problems (in this case, of living in a corrupt society) seem quite specific, but have a deep effect on the writer's relationships and personality: 'I am a secondary grade teacher, but have waited 4 years for work. It is the fifth year now without work — it affects my spiritual peace. There is no work in the Government Panchayat School without paying a bribe. It is a sin to give, but there is no work. My parents are on in years. I want to relieve the family burden. My parents say "How long should we keep you if you won't find and give money to get a job." Jesus so far has been my helper and my all-sufficiency. My daily prayer is, "Lord take me before I am forced to give money." My mind is disturbed. Please pray for me and my family.'

Some letters raise so many issues that it must be very difficult to know just where to begin in replying to them. A doctor writes: 'I was greatly encouraged to hear you say over the radio that you were willing to pray for those that had problems. I am not well and request you to please pray for me. Also, please send me the addresses of any of the authentic Christian healers who will pray for me and send me prayer cloths. Especially the address of Oral Roberts and T. L. Osborne. I am 49 years old and was converted in 1948 but did not stay with the Lord and only came back in 1973. I feel that I have lost the best and greater part of my life and would like to go on with the Lord at least now at this very late stage . . . I feel that I am clinging to Him because of my prayers and meditation and my listening to FEBC and FEBA. But true faith means that I realise that it is He who saves me and keeps me safe. That He has me in His hand and not I who keep Him by my efforts. Could you help me?'

Quite a number of letters, such as this one from a Muslim country, are written against a background of persecution: 'Praise to Him who put faith in my heart. Praise to the Lord Jesus who through His power my heart was enlightened although I was born in a far place from that where His message was established. Dear Brethren I have read quite a few Christian books but that is not enough. Please send me the Bible because I want to memorise it if possible during the summer vacation.

Write me during summer only because it is very risky to write during the school year. I was kicked out of school because of the books of Christ which I read for the students. The teacher was mad at me and caused my expulsion. Also don't write your address on the envelope in order they might not be able to tell that it is coming from you. A group of religious leaders in collaboration with the post office have taken note of this. Are you intending on establishing a religious (Christian) school in one of the nearby cities for teaching the Bible? If so, please send me the address in order to join it at the end of this school year. But if you have not thought of such a school, you must start one, and I will help you as much as I can.'

Replying to letters such as have been quoted is obviously an immense responsibility. What qualities are required for this work? Leoda Buckwalter lists seven: (1) Personal experience of the Lord Jesus Christ; this is basic and fundamental. (2) A good grasp of the Scriptures. (3) Spiritual discernment and empathy of spirit. (4) Prayer concern for the person who has written in — much more than a job. (5) Maturity produced by personal experience of trials and sufferings, endured victoriously. (6) The ability to keep confidence about matters entrusted to correspondence. (7) The right choice of aids — the proper tract, etc.

She also underlines the need for knowledge of the reception area. 'Problems here have their own emphasis — how to live in a joint-family system, or with the mother-in-law in the home; how to choose a husband or wife; how to find the will of God, especially if your parents refuse to allow you to do what you feel the Lord desires. There are many more, so programming and follow-up must be relevant to the person in the culture and background which he represents.'

It is to be hoped that every programme-supplying agency includes sufficient men and women with this range of qualifications. But one suspects that workers of such maturity, perception and knowledge are liable to be 'promoted' to work that is 'more responsible'. A well-planned training programme seems essential for younger and inexperienced workers — but how often is training taken seriously?

Follow-up work makes considerable administrative dem-mands. A careful record must be kept of letters received; this provides the most reliable means of assessing the impact of a programme, and may be a useful source of information about reception. The transmitting station will also want to have figures showing letters received, as an index of the station's effectiveness.

Quite obviously, it is also important to keep records for each individual correspondent, so that such information is available as age, religion, language, reason for writing, frequency of letters. One programme supplier may do this by means of a simple ledger with a code for marking entries. A larger organisation may use a computer for this purpose, just like any big commercial undertaking.

One programme supplier at least uses the computer in writing follow-up letters. The machine is programmed with a number of different paragraphs, each designed for a specific need and class of recipient. From these, the follow-up worker selects whatever combination seems to offer most help to the correspondent. It is an ingenious way of saving time and readers will find it either appealing or appalling.

Literature is among the most important resources of the follow-up worker. The right book or pamphlet sent to a listener who is currently interested in its subject-matter can be (quite literally) of infinite value. A great deal is available, and the racks of literature displayed in a large follow-up department are as impressive as they are colourful, but unfortunately quantity alone is not enough, even when it is backed up by attractive production.

It is interesting, and even paradoxical, that the ministry of the *spoken* word is at this point hindered by the shortage of good *printed* material. There is far too little well-written literature produced by and for members of particular cultures and dealing realistically with problems important to them.

And, of course, even where material is available, there remains the problem of making the follow-up worker aware of its existence. You can't send a listener a pamphlet you've never heard of. FEBAI has found it possible to modify pamphlets produced in the west, in order to make them more suitable for Indian readers. They have published a tract of their own on smoking and have begun to compile a list of topics frequently mentioned by listeners, so that more tracts can be written by Indian writers.

Leoda Buckwalter has her own ideas about the use of literature: 'If the choice should be made between *letters* and *literature*, we would take personal letters for the work here in India, but we have seen the effectiveness of well-chosen literature to meet the need in hand. The other tendency is to use *literature* because of laziness — it takes more time and thought to write a pertinent letter! But when the two are joined intelligently, the most good is accomplished.' She goes on to quote an example: 'A young man, Hindu, in his late teens, has been writing to us for the past 1½ years and has been counselled by letters and literature. Now he gives a very clear witness of salvation and has been accepted into the FEBAI Fellowship on the recommendation of the follow-up staff, even though, as a minor, he can't take baptism and thus identify himself openly as a Christian. His work hinders him from listening to the radio more than about once a month so he is almost totally a product of well-handled follow-up.'

A story such as this will lead many readers to wonder why ever this correspondent was not put in touch with Christians in his neighbourhood. The same question could well be put in respect of many of the correspondents referred to earlier in this chapter. If they need human companionship, Christian fellowship and pastoral guidance, should these not be provided by the local church?

Sometimes this is done. A man who had become intensely discouraged and had tried to commit suicide, listened to the radio and wrote in. So a missionary was asked to visit him.

Subsequently the follow-up staff sent a donation of money to the missionary with the request that he buy food and deliver it to the family. This deeply touched them, and a genuine friendship has resulted over the last several years with the one who continues to bear this follow-up responsibility. The missionary on the spot has come and gone — the tie with FEBAI remains.

But it surely should be the rule, rather than the exception, that local Christians be responsible for follow-up. There must be a strong suspicion that failure to involve them in this is yet another example of missionary 'imperialism' or of the way in which clergy and 'full-time workers' undervalue the potential of 'laity'. After all, it's not as if the Christian church were a recent arrival, or an insignificant minority. Help must surely be available from that 2½ per cent, a total of over 12 millions?

There is certainly some force in this criticism, but not quite so much, perhaps, as may appear at first sight. (1) Much of the Indian church (like that in the west?) is spiritually half-dead and unlikely to be able to provide the sort of support required. (2) Christians are very unevenly distributed throughout the country and there are in fact large areas with very few indeed. (3) There is a social and educational difficulty; it would often be difficult to match correspondents with neighbouring counsellors for age, sex, education and general cultural background. (4) Sadly, denominational differences are a significant barrier. (5) Communication is often difficult.

Once more, Leoda Buckwalter speaks from direct experience and with an admission of personal failure: 'In the case of non-Christians, we find several difficulties. Many resent personal visits from local Christians since this points up their interest in Christianity and invites hostility from their relatives and friends. In India the joint-family system is very strong, with many people living under one roof. Many young people listen alone, or with others of their age group, away from the family. One such radio club is found in W. Bengal where 30 young men in their teens are listening daily and sending in reception reports. Some have made a profession of faith. To such, a personal visit might well be disastrous. However, we rely heavily on the radio programmes themselves to strengthen faith and to give nurture to those who listen. Also, radio rallies and occasionally a visit to the area by the radio personnel themselves have been much appreciated and give the listener an opportunity to declare his love for the Lord Jesus. Otherwise he relies on *letterature*!

'Personal experience (when failing to carry out follow-up in Delhi, a city of several million people, with poor public transport, and after an already loaded day in the office) has shown me the futility of expecting busy pastors and local believers to do very much about following up people in their own areas. We have tried, but had little or no success! In my case, I merely could refer the person to someone working with that particular type of individual, e.g. nurses, university students, etc.'

Follow-up workers can tell stories which are both amusing and amazing. For amusement, consider the trained nurse who, with her husband, was seconded by BMMF to work at the Delhi office of FEBAI. Between August and November 1973 she answered several highly literate letters from a man who was interested in reading, doing correspondence courses (24 of them by January 1974, meriting 17 certificates). He distributed programme guides to others in the government establishment that he wrote from, and she sent him a booklet on how to run a cell group.

It was only after writing in April 1974 about his conversion a few months previously that he made clear that his presence at the prison was due not to his working as a governor or prison officer but to having been convicted in connection with the murder of a government official. And this was the man who had been told how to run a 'cell' group!

Amusing, certainly, but heart-warming too. This 'prodigal son' of a prosperous Brahmin family (his father a doctor, one brother an army major and one a high-ranking civil servant) now wrote: 'Since I have received Jesus in my heart as Lord and Saviour, I know where I have come from, I know why I am here and I know where I am going and I have now peace in my heart . . . Above all I want to be an effective and powerful witness.'

The following may serve as an example of the amazing stories. One broadcaster received a letter from a young woman telling of trouble between her brother and his wife, the brother religious and the wife 'a worldly woman.' Would he please write to the brother and counsel him? The name was familiar — brother and broadcaster had not only attended the same classes as students, but had even shared a hostel room for two years!

Such stories are exceptional, of course, although — human nature being what it is — they are the ones that feature in reports and at deputation meetings. It is no less true in the field of Christian broadcasting than in other areas that a sensational story laced with the right dash of pious sentiment works wonders in eliciting what is sometimes called 'practical fellowship'. For some people, emotion appears to be the only factor in Christian giving; they are more hard-headed when they buy a car or groceries.

Most follow-up work is routine and unspectacular. Few people think of it or pray for it. There is something dynamic about the vision of engineers building a transmitter station and aerial array. There is drama even in servicing the generators and nursing the transmitters. The broadcaster in front of the microphone 'bringing the word of life to Christless millions' may seem (in imagination at least) a heroic figure. But who remembers or prays for routine work at the follow-up interface where personal contact with listeners takes place? Paul may have been the first Christian to write letters to the glory of God. Happily, he was not the last.

[*Although most of the letters quoted in this chapter were prompted by broadcasts from FEBA Seychelles, some come from other sources, including Radio ELWA.*]

CHAPTER 9

Is Anybody Listening?

WHETHER A BUSINESS deals in breakfast food or machine tools, there is one question it dare not overlook. 'Who needs the product?' 'Whom are we selling to?' Ignore this, and you find yourself trying to market ham in Israel, fur coats in Singapore, freezer units in Siberia. Hence the need for what is called market research.

There are, of course, important differences between marketing a product and broadcasting the message of the Bible, but Christian radio can scarcely do without audience research. At a very simple level, audience research may help to avoid the danger of 'household hints' including pork recipes for Muslims and beef recipes for Hindus. At a more sophisticated level, teaching about the deity of Christ will vary according to its audience; Muslims, who believe passionately that God is a solitary unit, have different problems from Hindus who, believing that deity manifests itself in innumerable gods and goddesses, find no difficulty in adding 'Jesus' to that number.

A programme designed for a rural village audience should differ from one intended for more sophisticated urban listeners. Every secular station in the world adapts its programmes to the interests or needs of its listeners.

Christian communicators cannot afford to overlook these factors. Ralph Milton, in *Radio Programming* (Bles:London 1968) points out that the broadcaster must aim to meet the listener's *needs* by providing a programme that the listener *likes* and expresses this visually:

YOUR MESSAGE	uses—	PROGRAMMES THE LISTENER LIKES	to meet—	THE LISTENER'S NEEDS

Gaining this sort of knowledge demands time and hard work. Even broadcasters living in the reception area may need help — for example, the urban second-generation Christian graduate may not understand the world of the Hindu villager even if he speaks the same language. And trivial details can be important — as in the case of the health education programme which initially used for its signature tune a melody that proved to be associated in the reception area with the encouraging words, 'I am not afraid to die'!

Understanding the culture of the people they are trying to help is a task that all missionaries (as well as social workers) have to face. But broadcasting makes a further demand. After a programme has been planned with the needs of the audience in mind, the question remains — how effective was it? Could it be heard in the reception area? If so, did anybody listen to it?

The 'marketing' analogy helps to show one reason why these questions are so important. After hundreds of thousands of pounds have been spent on a new product in identifying a need, designing the product, putting it into production and advertising its existence, any business that wants to stay solvent will try to find out who are buying the product, who are not attracted by it, and the reasons influencing each group.

Christian broadcasting also costs a lot of money. It is intended to lead listeners to faith in Christ, or to help Christians become more like Jesus. Individual programmes are designed to achieve these objectives with respect to specific kinds of listeners. The question must be faced: is this money being wisely spent? Is it achieving the intended purpose? Or might the Christians all over the world who give so generously to Christian radio be just as well advised to pour it down the drain?

There are several 'easy' ways of answering these questions. None of them is satisfactory. Some broadcasters allow themselves to be encouraged by the approval of *people they meet.* It doesn't need much thought to see why such comments are worthless as a means of assessing audience response. Most of us prefer saying pleasant things to being negative and what could be more natural when meeting a broadcaster whose programme one heard three months ago than to say: 'Oh yes, I *did* enjoy your programme when I heard it recently!'

Even if the encouragement comes from *a regular listener*, he may not be the type whom the programme is supposedly intended to reach. Why should it be encouraging to know that 'You Need Christ', said to be an evangelistic programme for teenagers, is never missed by Colonel R. Postlethwaite or Mavis M. Mimms, both saved forty years ago? (On second thoughts, there could be reasons — they both pray regularly. And send gifts for 'the work'.)

It's absurd to attach great importance to the reactions of *individuals met socially*, because the people who meet Christian broadcasters are not typical of the target audience. A better guide may be the comments of *missionaries, clergy and other Christians* who meet listeners casually and feed back their comments. Perhaps more help may be available in *listeners' letters?* These obviously come from a wide variety of people who actually hear the programme, and who often comment on its value. If their reactions are sifted and classified, they can be put to good use in planning future programmes.

But the sifting and classification are absolutely essential. We are brought back to the basic issue of the target audience. How many letters come from listeners in this category? If you are trying to reach non-Christian students, it is not really very encouraging to discover that most of the letters come from middle-aged church members. In any case, even the letters sent by the target audience will not convey an accurate picture of audience response, for two reasons that are obvious — once they have been seen!

The first is that letters come only from members of a group which, in the Third World at least, is rather limited — viz. those who can both write and afford to buy a stamp for their letter. Given the low literacy rates and the equally low earnings in much of the Third World, it is clear that, even allowing for cases where a family or other group writes jointly, letters will tend to represent the opinions of the educated and (comparatively) prosperous.

Secondly, letters tend to be favourable. Writing a letter takes effort, time and money. People are far more likely to expend these in order to encourage an activity of which they approve than to enjoy the doubtful pleasure of being rude.

In other words, the poor and the uneducated, the hostile and the bored, don't write letters.

While we are coming to terms with this rather daunting subject — the difficulty of knowing who (if anybody) is listening to programmes — we might mention a particularly glaring type of wishful thinking occasionally practised by Christian broadcasters.

The formula to beware goes like this: 'Every day *x* programmes are relayed to *y* listeners over an area of *z* million square miles.'

Let's start with the *range*. Of course short-wave transmitters have a phenomenal range, but the areas of *good* reception where serious listening is possible cannot be easily calculated. Atmospheric conditions, 'spots' on the sun, and many other factors make this sort of calculation unrealistic.

How about the *number* of listeners? First of all, what is a 'listener'? We must admit that there are many different levels of listening — of five people in a room with a radio playing, two may be consciously listening, two barely hearing, and one fast asleep. Secondly, no Christian radio outfit can afford the sampling techniques employed by agencies such as the BBC when they want to establish listener figures. (They select a sample reproducing as accurately as possible the different social classes in the population and question each member of this carefully chosen sample about what programmes they have heard in the period being considered). When a Christian radio station or programme claims to have *y* million listeners, the figure is decided in one of the following ways. (All are inadequate.)

The figure may refer to the total population in the area, i.e. to the potential audience (including young children?) Obviously this is completely unrealistic. No programme in Great Britain has 50 million listeners, even if this is the size of the population.

Alternatively the figure may be the number of radio sets in the area (possibly multiplied by two or three to allow for the cases where several people listen together). This may seem a more reputable basis to use, but it still won't do. Are the programmes being transmitted on short waves? If so, how many of the sets are able to receive them? Short-wave sets cost more than medium-wave and although in some large states they form a relatively higher proportion of the total number of sets than in (for example) the UK they are still only a proportion. In any case, why say *y* million listeners if you mean that number of assorted radios, some of which can't receive the programmes?

What about the number of programmes? It sounds very impressive to say that *x* thousand programmes go out each month. But if we look more closely at the programmes we see that many are repeated. So *x* thousand doesn't mean that number of *different* programmes. Then we notice the number of languages being used. Not one of our *y* million 'listeners' can understand *all* these programmes. Many of them can follow only the tiny proportion in their own language. They may represent several million of the global 'listener' figure but they can make sense of (perhaps) only five programmes per week — if reception is good enough.

The story of Christian radio is sufficiently exciting and inspiring not to need the sort of publicity that would be disallowed by any reputable advertising standards bureau. Does its use perhaps indicate a lack of self-confidence in those who resort to it? Or does it derive from fear that the Christian public is still sceptical about radio work?

Phil Booth of Radio Worldwide makes a similar point in *Slim Fingers* (Christian Literature Crusade, Fort Washington, 1976, p. 88): 'When will we learn, as Christian broadcasters, that population, potential audience, and real audience are not the same thing? The population of India is about 600 million. But the potential audience for Christian programmes is limited to those who have access to short-wave radios[1], and that number is again reduced to an even smaller real audience which is interested enough in "my" programme to stay tuned. This is not to belittle the significance of the true potential audience: it is making a plea for realistic thinking and more truth in promotional statements.'

That last phrase is a key one. Most potential supporters find it far more encouraging to be told 'Your money is helping us to reach millions of listeners' than 'We want to spend some of the money you send in an attempt to find out who actually are listening.'

Audience research does, after all, cost money. It also demands a good deal of time which is an even scarcer commodity. The temptation is great to ignore this need and to go on broadcasting 'in faith' — although to use *that* word for such an ostrich-head-in-the-sand attitude is bizarre.

In India, some audience research has been done by a non-religious body. The Indian Institute of Public Opinion (IPO) works on the well-known Gallup Poll principle of questioning a random sample (carefully matched to the population as a whole). Since 1960 the IPO has carried out repeated surveys on various aspects of broadcasting, such as the pattern of radio listening, listening hours, programme preference, and the image of All-India Radio. (All-India Radio itself has done surveys but the results of these are not published.) In general the surveys have been limited to four large cities, Bombay, Calcutta, Madras and New Delhi; only one survey has been

1. Correct when *Slim Fingers* was written.

conducted in villages and small towns, although the greater part of the population lives in these. The 1971 figures showed that 66 per cent of respondents in small towns listened to the radio, and 57 per cent in rural areas. By contrast, a 1973 survey in the cities mentioned showed 92 per cent listening.

An alternative to the rather expensive method of random sampling a large population would be to concentrate attention on the individuals actually known to listen to programmes. Researching the nature and interests of the *known* audience might be equally as valuable as trying to discover its extent.

Is there any way of identifying and contacting the audience? One obvious answer is to get in touch with people who have written about programmes. A good deal of Christian radio research has been done on this basis, which does obviously ensure contact with actual listeners. Unfortunately, as we have seen, the listeners who write in are by no means typical of the audience as a whole, and this fact casts some doubt upon the validity of any survey based on follow-up files. There is another difficulty; it has been found in practice that a significantly large number of programme suppliers do not record names and addresses with sufficient care to justify using these for research.

After three years of broadcasting, FEBA felt in 1973 that the time had come for a serious attempt to find out who were listening to their programmes. The letters processed at Bangalore showed some significant and surprising tendencies. Anne Ediger, at that time a FEBC worker and research co-ordinator for FEBAI, who carried out the research we are about to describe, summarises these tendencies in an unpublished MA thesis, from which this chapter quotes freely.

Over three successive years, 81.25 per cent of feedback came from Christians who comprise only 2.6 per cent of the total population. Hindus, who constitute 82.72 per cent of India's total population, comprised 15.66 per cent of the listener response, and Moslems, constituting 11.21 per cent of the total population, comprised only 1.25 per cent of the response.

'Several other striking facts showed up, for example, the high response from students — In some instances, response came from a completely different group than the producer had set as his target. Response to different languages differed significantly numerically. It was found that far more response came from South India than from North India, Telegu and Tamil rating highest. Hindi, the national language, came out with a relatively low mail response.'

FEBC-Manila and FEBAI-Bangalore had already experienced difficulty in previous surveys. When in 1963 FEBC sent out 12,000 questionnaires to listeners on their mailing list in Asian countries, only 8.6 per cent were returned. A FEBA postcard survey in 1969 had produced a better proportional response (22.5 per cent of the cards were returned) but the basis of the research was limited (8,000 cards went out to the *English* mailing list).

The 1973 research project focussed on listeners in four major language groups: Hindi, English, Telegu and Tamil. Hindi is the 'official' language; English is the common 'second' language; Tamil and Telegu are widely spoken and programmes in them draw a high response.

Listeners were to be contacted by means of spot announcements on FEBA-Seychelles and FEBC-Manila offering a free pennant. (The pennant in fact was a triangle of fabric, about nine inches long, bearing the words FEBA-I and 'The fear of the Lord is the beginning of wisdom'.) The pennant, spoken of in the announcements as suitable for decorating a wall, would hopefully elicit 1,000 responses, more or less (say 900–1,400), in each language group. Should larger numbers respond, a random sample would be taken, so that numbers in each group might be broadly comparable. This incentive was intentionally modest. Not only were funds limited; a more impressive gift would have prompted a less useful response. Voice of America discovered this when it offered radios in 1968, with the result that listeners filled in questionnaires for whole families and relatives, even making their own copies of the questionnaire for the purpose!

Information about listeners responding was to be obtained by a mailed questionnaire. Alternative methods (telephone interview, personal interview) were ruled out because of the wide area to be covered and the high cost they would entail.

As requests for the pennant came in, several steps were taken. (1) Checks were made to ensure that no respondent was represented more than once. (2) A questionnaire was sent out with each pennant, together with a return envelope, post paid. (3) Respondents also received a letter explaining the purpose of the questionnaire and mentioning that alarm clocks would be sent to five selected respondents who returned completed questionnaires.

The Tamil and English responses were swift, soon securing 1,391 and 2,434 answers respectively. In order to limit numbers, only one out of two of the English answers were selected for use in the survey. After a longer period, Telegu responses came to 1,097 and Hindi totalled 1,127. Responses from outside India were not analysed, and all were carefully screened to ensure that they came from actual listeners.

A total of 4,832 questionnaires was distributed. Of these 3,430 were returned, representing a 71 per cent response. This figure conceals substantial differences between language groups, which responded as follows:

Telegu	77%	Tamil	82%
Hindi	60%	English	65%

It is a satisfactory response in comparison with the usually low level associated with postally administered questionnaires. But before looking at the findings of the survey, it may be wise to indicate what it did not (try to) achieve.

Because it concentrated upon people who actually listen to the programmes, it inevitably has nothing to say about those who do not; yet these are arguably a far more important group and a great deal of work must be put into attracting their interest. Linked with this point is another — that the survey is largely concerned with the views of Christians. The proportions were as follows:

Language	% Christians
Telegu	79
Tamil	89
Hindi	52
English	83

Now it is certainly of value to know that almost the whole of the audience for Telegu, Tamil and English language programmes is Christian and no doubt the Hindi programmers took note of the difference in their situation — but these helpful findings underline the need to be clear about what sort of information is *not* available from the survey results.

Some facts that did become clear:

1. The most popular listening times are 6–9 a.m. and 6–10 p.m.
2. Weekend listening is very popular, especially on Sundays.
3. Many people listen in groups of six or more (i.e. the whole family together).
4. Listeners are above average educationally — most have been to high school or college.
5. Christian teaching programmes and devotional music are very popular; likewise drama and news.
6. Good news programmes are appreciated.
7. Radio Ceylon is very popular.
8. 56 per cent of listeners found FEBA or FEBC by accident (some were told by friends).

In the light of these and other facts that emerged, Anne Ediger made a series of recommendations, summarised and discussed below:

1. *Since the majority of the present FEBC/FEBA listenership is comprised of Christians, programming needs to be thoroughly overhauled and specific steps taken to programme for the non-Christian, if FEBC/FEBA aims to reach this community as well.*

On the face of it, the survey has disclosed a rather shocking state of affairs. Hundreds of thousands of pounds are being spent on what is supposed to be evangelism — yet more than three-quarters of the listeners are Christians. But there are one or two points to consider before writing off the whole Christian radio enterprise as yet another example of Christians devoting vast amounts of time and money for the pleasure of talking to themselves.

First, it may well be that, bad as the record is, FEBA/FEBC is at least no worse than other agencies in this respect. If a 77 per cent Christian audience is to be regarded as unacceptable, then Christians should probably scrap not only radio outreach but also evangelistic rallies so as to concentrate on personal evangelism.

Second, something may be thought to depend on the *size*, not just the composition of the listenership. Twenty-three per cent of India's unbelievers would represent a remarkable audience for evangelism and might well be thought to justify the enterprise. If, in addition, a large number of Christians listen, then this fact in no way negates the achievement of reaching so many non-Christians.

Third, it's fair to ask what sort of Christians the 77 per cent may be. For many Indians, as for many in the west, the word implies mere membership of a community (not even, perhaps, of a local church) and says nothing about genuine personal discipleship and commitment. Nominal Christianity is scandal all over the world. Such 'Christians' need evangelising every bit as much as their 'non-Christian' fellows.

Fourth, there is evidence that Christians who have benefited from Christian radio programmes can be very effective in evangelising their neighbours.

All the same, the recommendation is urgent; it seems clear that FEBA/FEBC (like the church as a whole) is at present failing to attract the attention of non-Christians.

2, 3. *As the largest single group of listeners consists of students between 17 and 20, with 44 per cent of the total having high school and 39 per cent some university education, a concerted effort should be made to produce programmes aimed at this group.*

Yes, of course — for a variety of reasons most programme suppliers are too frightened or too lacking in intellectual resources to provide programmes which will present Christianity as intellectually reputable and relevant to the latter part of the twentieth century. Here, as in other respects, evangelicals in India seem to stand more or less where western evangelicals stood in the 1930s. But having said this, it must be admitted that the present programmes do apparently appeal to better-educated listeners. Perhaps the answer is that improved programmes would reach more *non-Christians* in this category, an objective which FEBC/FEBA must surely take seriously.

4, 5. *In view of the evidence about listening times, programmes should, so far as possible, be transmitted at peak listening hours, and programmes should be devised for weekend listening.*

6. *Since the sample shows language preference in the order English, Hindi, Tamil, Telegu, more time and attention should be given to programming in English and Hindi. But this must not mean using (for example) increasing numbers of programmes planned originally for British and North American audiences; programming must be done by people familiar with Indian culture.*

7. *FEBA should establish its own news service, measuring up to BBC credibility.*

In view of what has been said elsewhere (pp. 69f., 72f.,) about the importance of a news service, this recommendation needs little discussion. Its implementation is described on pp. 74f.

8. *In devising new programmes, care should be taken to include some that appeal to the whole family, to provide for the needs and interests of women and children, to make greater use of drama (especially, though not exclusively, in programmes aimed at youth) and to offer more music and song, including devotional song.*

9. *New types of programme should be introduced in an attempt to create new interest and draw new listeners. Some examples:*

general knowledge; English teaching; quiz programmes with listener participation; educational programmes; stories.

10. *More care should be taken with the 'language-style' of the programmes. This means not only paying attention to the intonation, phrasing and modulation of speakers (i.e. what they sound like) but also choice of words and expressions, and use of 'local colour' and illustrations (i.e. what they actually say).*

Recommendations 8–10 entail the appointment of new specialised staff (full or part-time) with creative ability to develop the new programmes that are needed.

This is an important and rather controversial suggestion. It is quite obvious that many *programme suppliers* are neither able nor willing to work along the lines suggested in 8–10. They do not have workers with these skills. They may not be convinced of the value of the 'secular' programmes required. If they had more money and more workers and more skill, they might well prefer to devote these to the direct 'preaching of the gospel' which is, in any case, what most of their (financial and prayer) supporters are interested in.

The implication is that FEBA must accept the responsibility. This sounds straight forward enough, but may not be so easy in practice. It means spending more money, at a time when inflation is threatening much Christian work, and spending it in a way that many will see as non-productive. It means that FEBA will become more of a programme-supplying and perhaps, less of an 'enabling' agency i.e. one that exists in order to serve other agencies by transmitting programmes they have produced.

11. *Continued efforts must be made to get a clear signal.* This calls for yet more work by the technical experts on Mahé. But it is absolutely critical. One of the most frequent suggestions for increasing the audience is to advertise. But advertising a programme or station is largely useless unless people responding to the publicity can be sure of hearing the programme clearly. Until this condition is met, advertising means throwing money away. Of course highly motivated listeners, isolated

Christians, for example, will listen very faithfully even to a bad signal, but their case is very different from that of the comparatively uninterested listener whom it is hoped to attract by advertising. The order must be first, a clear signal; second, carefully planned publicity. Happily, the reef aerial project (chapter 4) has achieved the first goal.

12. *More audience research is called for. Areas to be surveyed should include: high school and college students generally (i.e. not merely those who listen to FEBA); the 'man in the street' who seems largely untouched by the present programmes; the Moslem community.*

Obviously the findings of such research would be useful to all Christian agencies working in this field, and it would be reasonable for as many as possible to co-operate in the surveys. (Unhappily, radio work shows as many signs of competition as of co-operation between Christian bodies, cf. pp. 135ff.)

There can be no doubting the importance of audience research, even though financing it calls for faith and integrity from those who devote to this purpose money which some fellow-Christians may feel could be better spent on direct evangelisation and Christian teaching. Even when such research has been done (and FEBA deserves credit for what has been undertaken) the results may not be wholly encouraging and may point to a need for further expenditure. But honesty is no less important in serving God than it is in other areas of human life and there is nothing at all to be said for the pious ostriches of Christian broadcasting who are content to spend lavishly on westernised 'Bible-based' programmes without bothering to find out who is listening to them. No responsible secular body would act like this, and in undertaking research FEBA is taking the hint that Jesus dropped when he ruefully commented that 'the people of this world are . . . more shrewd than the people of the light' (Luke 16:8). To ignore audience research is not faith but foolishness.

CHAPTER 10

Money Well Spent?

CHRISTIAN RADIO WORK costs money. Some readers may be surprised to realise that the 1976/77 budget of FEBA, which is, after all, not a large organisation, exceeded £250,000.

What is the money spent on? In answering this question, it will be helpful to distinguish between the expenses involved in *supplying* and those incurred in *transmitting* programmes. FEBA, like the majority of transmitting agencies, does both, but most agencies involved in Christian radio work, including Back to the Bible, Hour of Decision and a host of smaller organisations, restrict themselves to programme supply.

Some expenses are common to both types of organisation. Among these we may mention:

1. *Living allowances or wages* for the workers who can't live on air, whether they are 'missionaries' or 'full-time workers' or simply employees. Some work is done by volunteers — in fact, the administration of FEBA at Woking has depended quite extensively on voluntary help — but this represents only a fraction of the work force.

2. *Rent, rates, and maintenance* of buildings is another unavoidable expense. They may be insignificant for a programme made in a 'studio' at the end of somebody's garden or in a room on a Bible college campus. But renting premises in a large city may be very expensive and building your own studio and offices is also costly.

3. *Postage* is another substantial item. The greater the number of letters received, the more it costs to answer them

(and, we may note in passing, the more people are needed for this work). In addition, tapes must be sent both to and from the transmitting station.

Programme suppliers are bound to spend a good deal on *tape*. This is a recurrent expense, and even if a supplier wishes to economise by re-using tape this may not be possible. It is illegal, for example, to return used tape from the Seychelles to India. Besides being recurrent, this expense has increased very sharply, being directly linked to the rising cost of oil, from which the tape is made.

Many programme suppliers also spend money on *artistes' fees* and expenses. This may surprise readers who assume that everybody providing material for a programme is a believer and works for nothing. Such an assumption is doubly mistaken. First, even Christians have to live; a full-time worker may be paid a fee, as he would for preaching in a church, and in any case will have expenses to meet. Second, some suppliers use non-Christian artistes especially to provide indigenous music; the musicians are sometimes willing to accept a fee far lower than normal since in India, for example, there is a great respect for religion, but nevertheless they must be paid.

Over and above these items, programme suppliers must find money to meet certain expenses which we consider elsewhere — *equipment, electricity, air time* and *monitoring charges.*

Before examining the expenses borne by a transmitter agency, it's worth pointing out that most of these also provide programmes, so that they too have to pay for tape, performing rights, and possibly artistes' fees. (FEBA, for example, has had to pay a good deal to provide a news service.)

The most obvious expense in running a transmitter (apart from those mentioned at 1 and 2 above) is the cost of *equipment*. Naturally a programme supplier has to buy some equipment, ranging from a modest professional tape recorder and microphone to expensive professional recorders and mixers. But the transmitting agency needs not only these but a great deal more very costly equipment. There must be a transmitter and aerials. The history of Christian radio is full of stories about how these have been picked up, against all the odds, at ridiculously low prices. For example there was the occasion when FEBC was offered a 300-foot steel tower for an aerial. The radio company that owned it had bought it for $3,700 and had paid $500 to ship it to Manila. FEBC got it for $300. Not long after, they were *given* a newly overhauled 30-kilowatt generator by a local broadcasting company. (No wonder the men and women who work in Christian radio believe in miracles!)

Yet in spite of such incidents the cost of equipping a transmitter station is high — to say nothing of the cost of servicing and up-dating it. FEBA paid £21,000 plus freight and import duty for their Gates transmitter, which was cheap since what they bought was the pre-production model. As for the reef aerial project — that cost £250,000. Valves, which have to be replaced regularly, may cost more than £1,500 each.

Electricity is another major item. Programme suppliers get electricity bills like the rest of us, but recorders use little power. The Gates transmitter, however, consumes 200 units per hour, a total of 730,000 units per year. (Just for comparison, a typical family in the UK might use 6,000 units). There are two ways of meeting this need, either by buying power the normal way from a local supplier or by purchasing generators and producing power on site. Here again rising oil prices are important; these soared by 75 per cent in one year and the local supplier very likely depends on oil, while on-site generators will almost certainly run on diesel fuel. During 1976/77, electricity cost FEBA over £30,000.

These facts explain what may seem a rather puzzling aspect of Christian radio finance — that Christian transmitting agencies charge Christian programme suppliers a fee for broadcasting their programmes. At first sight, this air-time payment seems absurd. Since both agencies are essential, and both serve the same cause, why ever should payment be required? The reason is not difficult to understand. The cost of transmitting is so great that part of it must be shouldered by the programme supplier. The programme supplier is in contact with a constituency made up of churches, agencies and individual Christians, who are not in direct touch with the radio station. They are nevertheless committed to the programmes produced, in respect of both prayer and financial support. As there would be little point in the supplier producing programmes if he were not able to broadcast them, and as he does not possess the means to broadcast them on his own, it is reasonable and even right for the broadcasting costs to be passed to the supplier by the station, so that they become part of the cost of the suppliers' ministry. At present, FEBA charges £24 per hour as the basic air time rate for a one transmitter service, adding a further £6 per hour for a two-transmitter service. This at-cost charge is related to running the station and certain administrative services but does not include the cost of FEBA personnel.

How does FEBA meet these costs? Some FEBA workers and supporters would be content to say simply that God supplies whatever is needed to do his will. 'Our Father pays the bills.' It would be wrong to ignore this way of looking at the problem of costs, for FEBA has in this sense most emphatically been a 'faith' mission, ever since the day described on p. 36 when the decision was taken to accept responsibility for broadcasting to India.

At that time FEBA was unknown, and it is still small by comparison with many missions. It is not financed by an industrial or commercial tycoon. Quite naturally, a Christian who examines the accounts and hears how the money has come in, is bound to feel that in some sense the 'pious' answer is the simple truth — that 'Our Father *does* pay the bills'.

From another viewpoint, however, Christian stewardship demands careful planning and attention to the way in which money is raised. Much comes from small donations, although there have been many occasions when a crisis has been averted by the arrival of a large gift — as when an anonymous gift of £5,000 arrived 'out of the blue'.

Impulse giving, however, is not a good basis for financial planning, and FEBA encourages supporters to give regularly. There is a programme sponsorship plan whereby supporters can (so to speak) 'buy' air time on behalf of programme suppliers who cannot afford the full cost themselves. One monthly unit of £2 finances five minutes of air time — less than many people pay for a very modest meal out.

A similar possibility of regular support is offered by 'missionary support units': regular payments of £1 per month for the duration of a three-four year tour of service and intended to help feed, clothe, and meet the other living costs of a particular worker. These payments are absolutely basic to FEBA financial policy. FEBA has no central fund designated for the paying of allowances to its missionaries, and the costs likely to be incurred whilst overseas must be covered by pledged support from Christians who remain at home. Paul and Barnabas were the only missionaries in their day, and the church at Antioch stood behind them as they went. Not every local church today can or will support everyone within its membership offering for service as a missionary. But up and down the country, there are hundreds of individual Christians who would dearly love to have a hand in supporting a specific missionary by name. These are people who would perhaps have wished to have gone to the field themselves, but they were not accepted; alternatively they are those who see their earning capacity as a means for sending others. Before any FEBA worker goes to Mahé he or she is required to have raised not only the cost of the (return!) fare, but also three-quarters of the first year's living allowance. An obvious way of doing this is by means of these missionary support units. There are possible objections to this FEBA policy. After all, if a FEBA selection panel takes a responsible decision that an individual is needed on Mahé, it seems only right that FEBA should accept responsibility for supporting the worker. On the other hand, it is urged that full-time Christian workers are 'sent' by churches who should also act responsibly by sharing the financial burden.

Generally speaking, the support originally offered is maintained and even increases.

There is clearly a danger that some missionaries may be better provided for than others, whose needs may be greater. This problem is not confined to FEBA; it is experienced wherever missionaries go, and is often solved spontaneously as missionaries share with each other. FEBA policy is to put all money received into an individual support account, from which payments are made to workers in accordance with a statutory rate of allowance. Individuals are sent copies of receipts issued to their personal supporters, together with monthly statements of their support accounts. But they receive funds only in the form of set allowances, whether or not their support fund is in credit.

In view of the expense of Christian radio, it is right to ask if there is no way of reducing costs. Certainly it's impossible to cut back on workers or on their allowances. Those on Mahé appear to be over-extended and they are in any case receiving much less than what they would earn, as qualified men and women, in government service, industry or commerce. Whatever may seem to be the case with some kinds of 'full-time Christian service', the activities of FEBA demand men and women of high professional calibre.

It has been suggested that Christian radio work should cease to focus on the provision of powerful transmitters and instead establish low-powered local stations. After all, it is urged, the pattern of secular broadcasting has changed in this way. Local stations, far from dying out in competition with national networks, have become more important. Christian local stations would be comparatively cheap to establish and, being staffed by local Christians, would communicate more effectively with local listeners.

This is an attractive prospect, offering greater effectiveness for a considerably lower cost. But there are many areas where it simply would not work; for example, in anti-Christian or rigorously 'secular' states; in states where there is a government radio monopoly, or in countries such as India where a high proportion of people live outside the big cities. So this approach could be used only in heavily urbanised nations, having an 'open market' in radio. In these circumstances, there is much to be said for it, provided the risk is accepted that a change in government policy might silence all (or all religious) independent radio stations. (It was such a change of policy that forced RVOG to close in 1977.) In which case, there would be a need for a large transmitter situated beyond the frontiers . . .

As for improving the quality of programmes, shortage of qualified local staff, and the difficulty many Christians have in relating to their own culture make it uncertain whether programmes would necessarily improve. The result might be that limited resources would lead to even more 'hymn and a thing' programming, or reliance on a stream of western evangelical/fundamentalist offerings: The Glory Hour, The Hiram Q. Bloggs Hour, Oldy Mouldies of Sacred Song, Scripture Skits and Washing through the Word. Just the same mixture, in fact, that already proclaims far and wide the western capitalist middle-class nature of the Christian message and its utter irrelevance to the problems of the twentieth century or the Third World. To establish small local stations would not in itself deal with this basic problem of programming.

Another suggested way of reducing costs is by using the transmitters of a commercial station. The simplest method is to buy air time, as many Christian organisations do on e.g. Radio Sri Lanka or Europe Number One. This has obvious advantages. It provides a ready-made audience, even if many of them are so bored by the Christian programmes that they simply switch off (for the experience of Radio Luxembourg, see p. 20). The benefits of transmitting on a well-known wavelength in the medium wave-band, and at high power are considerable; one agency receives far more letters through its Sri Lanka than from its Seychelles operations. (This may be explained in part by the fact that where a programme is available from two sources, interested listeners will choose the one with the more powerful signal.)

One disadvantage of using commercial transmitters is that the Christian message is likely to appear as one of many conflicting voices, including semi-Christian and non-Christian groups. Another is the impossibility of adequate programming; all that the commercial station can offer is an isolated fifteen- or thirty-minute slot, often at a time unsuitable for listeners, with the programme supplier having no control over what precedes or follows his programme. In addition, a commercial station may change its policy for sound commercial reasons, and leave the Christian agencies using it without any outlet. The case of Radio Luxembourg has already been mentioned and it is significant that Radio Sri Lanka's decision to permit religious broadcasts arose from a shortage of foreign currency.

Page 26 describes the kind of arrangement TWR has made in Monte Carlo and later in Sri Lanka. This way of securing facilities has advantages and defects; elsewhere TWR has built its own station; it serves to emphasise the point that there are more ways than one of maintaining a Christian radio ministry.

Quite plainly, costs will continue to rise. Inflation will see to that. In addition, as the work becomes more effective it is bound to expand as more letters are received and more opportunities present themselves. It is impossible to avoid wondering whether the large sums needed might not be more usefully spent in other ways.

The easy, 'pious' answer is to say that 'if one soul is saved, then no expenditure is too great.' This is a very effective defence against criticism, for it leaves the objector apparently suggesting that the salvation of an individual is *not* worth so much. But in fact the alternatives are not so simple. The question to be answered is not whether one conversion is worth £*x*,000 but whether £*x*,000 might not have been spent in *n* ways that would have resulted in *more* conversions. Specifically, in the present context, should not the vast sums being spent on Christian radio be allocated instead to more traditional and possibly more economical forms of outreach?

It is a plausible argument, but before accepting it, we must consider two points. First of all, Christians tend to be complacent about the cost-effectiveness of traditional methods. They under-estimate the amount spent by local churches and other evangelistic agencies and take it for granted that these are effective. But even if doubts about the second assumption are ignored, it cannot be denied that the cost of running a local church is considerable. Over and above the capital investment required, heating, lighting, maintenance, salary for clergy and caretaker, purchasing items (from hymnbooks to instant coffee) required for the activities of the church — all these add up to a sizeable bill. Multiply it by the number of churches involved and the total is formidable. In *Ears that Hear* (Radio Worldwide, London 1966, p. 14) Phil Booth concludes that 'if the expenses of the average church are worked out . . . and then this figure be equated to the number of hours ministry each week to the average number of people attending the meetings — it will be found that money spent *wisely* on radio is, by comparison, a very economic means of spreading the Gospel.'

Secondly, it seems that in some cases there is no alternative to using radio, whatever the expense. 'All nations' in Matt. 28: 19 includes those which cannot be evangelised by other means. Some are dominated by ideologies, religious or secular, which hinder or even prohibit Christian proclamation; some are experiencing an increase in population so explosive that traditional methods are inadequate. So far as these are concerned, criticism of the expense of establishing radio stations is irrelevant. Evangelism has to be done this way or not at all.

In addition, there is a more radical criticism of spending money on Christian radio. Millions of undernourished and diseased members of the family of man surely need material help, not disembodied radio preaching? Relief organisations are constantly appealing for help and Christians are becoming more and more aware of their responsibility to care for men's bodies as well as their souls.

Three things need to be said about this. The first is that caring for spiritual and physical needs are not alternatives. Christians can and should do both. It is not a case of either/or but both/and.

Secondly, there are signs that some Christians are in danger of losing their commitment to relieve spiritual deprivation. It is far easier to raise a million pounds for agricultural projects, which all men and women of good will regard as their duty, than to collect the same amount for distributing the Bible, which is the responsibility of Christians alone. As Jesus said in a rather different context: This you should have done and not left the other undone.

Thirdly, and perhaps most important, saving men's souls often has remarkable effects in reducing social and physical suffering. It could be argued that one of the greatest needs of the Third World is for more Christian men and women committed in Christ to work and fight and care for their fellows. Relief agencies have the greatest difficulty in finding nationals who are proof against corruption and willing to administer aid disinterestedly. If there is a decline in living faith among western nations, then one sign will be an increase in corruption and a decrease in the numbers of men and women willing to give time and labour to serving others in need.

Reading a list of relief agencies operating in Bombay was an interesting experience. The list was comprehensive, but the organisations named were overwhelmingly Christian. India, like other nations, desperately needs the sort of Christian humanitarian grass-roots concern that characterised Victorian Britain. But this concern arises directly from the experience of new birth and a life of discipleship to Jesus.

It is hard to exaggerate the potential of Christian radio in this context. The Christian Welfare Society of Madras shows how spiritual renewal and social concern go together. Its founder is a company secretary, a gently spoken member of the Roman Catholic community. It was 'by chance' that he heard a broadcast from the Seychelles and ultimately came to see Christianity in a new light. He listened to programmes in Tamil, Telegu and English. His new faith changed his life. Whereas previously the day's work left him so exhausted that when he returned home he could do little more than lie back with his feet up, a personal relationship with Jesus Christ filled him with vitality. He realised that he had been ignoring the needs of others, and became surprised and ashamed at how easy it is, as he explains, 'to give God only one's second-best'. He saw the truth of 1 John 4:20, 21 — that the man who does not show love for his neighbour proves that he does not love God. He became involved with the social work, house visitation and Bible distribution of the Catholic Social Welfare Committee. He even founded an organisation to help the poor of Madras — and was shocked at the reluctance of his prosperous friends to donate 50 rupees per year for humanitarian work. Simultaneously he became increasingly conscious of a need for systematic and solid personal Bible study. This may surprise people who believe in an either/or relationship between theology and action, but the Bible and Christian experience show clearly that the peculiar weapon of the Christian church in fighting against human need is the preaching, not of a narrowly-defined 'gospel', but of the whole word of God.

There is no reason to think that if Christian radio ceased tomorrow there would be any more money available to help the Third World. Many supporters would decide to send their gifts to other evangelistic agencies. Whereas it is quite certain that if the church gave up its work of evangelising, the Third World would (simply from a human viewpoint) be deprived of a constant supply of revitalised men and women.

We have already seen why the population explosion makes radio an indispensable means of evangelising the world. As Paul Freed of TWR points out, it is not the only means but it is an essential one. 'The message never changes from one century to another. That hard plodding, going down into the village, talking face to face with people, establishing the local church, must never stop. But we do need to catch a vision that we are losing ground — every day, every week, every month, every year. Christian broadcasting is not the only answer. It is only a small part of the total outreach — radio, literature, audio-visuals, missionary aviation, translations, programmed instruction are all new ways in which we can move out in geometric proportions. We need a continually renewed vision of ways to reach others. Compared to the rest of the world's progress, Christendom is dragging at a snail's pace. I must make it very clear, though, that winning people to Christ will require both methods, the personal touch and the mass media'.[1]

In the last resort, the decision about allocating money to Christian radio will not depend simply on a rational evaluation of the comparative merits of material aid, Bible translation projects, and church growth campaigns. Broadcasting is one way — in the twentieth century, an essential way — of obeying the command to 'go into all the world and preach the gospel'. Where Christians are convinced that God is leading them to share in this way of doing his work they will give what they can.

1. *Towers to Eternity* (Word Books, Waco, Texas, 1968), p. 88.

CHAPTER 11

Business or Mission?

'I SOMETIMES WONDER,' said the FEBA worker, 'whether we are a business run by missionaries or a mission run by businessmen.' The remark may shock people who know little about Christian broadcasting or the work of missionary societies. Surely missionaries should not talk so cynically, and if they do are not their words best forgotten?

Yet the comment points to a whole series of problems which affect FEBA, some of them common to many organisations connected with Christian radio, and some, in fact, shared by all missionary societies. They are no less important for being so rarely discussed that the average praying and giving supporter does not even realise they exist. We mention them now, so that people may think and pray more realistically about organisations with which they are involved. It's often necessary to identify problems in order to focus prayer.

More than once already we have found it helpful to compare the work of Christian radio organisations to a business. Obviously there are big differences in the objectives of a business and a mission, but some programme suppliers as well as some transmitting agencies do show a very shrewd concern for finance. Although their purpose is not to make a profit, many Christian missions, not just those involved in radio work, cannot help resembling businesses to a remarkable degree.

They dispose of large sums of money. We refer to the budget of FEBA elsewhere, but this is peanuts by comparison with that of organisations such as TWR or HCJB, or a mission like the

CMS. These funds must not only be raised but allocated and doing this demands shrewd and responsible decision-making.

They are responsible for activities which are often wide-ranging (in geography and kind) and often highly complex. So far as geography is concerned, even FEBA, which is by no means large, operates in two centres in India (FEBAI) one in Pakistan, one in East Africa, besides the base at Mahé and the office at Woking. The activities include building, civil engineering, electronic engineering and maintenance, producing and transmitting radio programmes (including a news service), administering air time, public relations, staff recruitment, providing a pastoral and advisory service for listeners, and all the secretarial and administrative machinery needed to facilitate these enterprises. Again we note that such variety and complexity are not peculiar to FEBA, nor even to Christian radio organisations.

It follows naturally that *a variety of skilled workers is needed.* The story told in earlier chapters makes this abundantly clear. Everything has depended on having workers with the right qualifications and experience available at the right time. Failure to see what posts must be filled when and to secure suitable candidates would cripple the whole enterprise. And, of course, the larger organisations have 'pay-rolls' that are quite sizeable by business standards.

Although Christian organisations may not appear to have a 'board of directors' yet somewhere within them there must be *a body which makes the same sort of policy decisions (future projects, allocation of resources) as are made in the business world by the board.* Quite often it is the 'council' or the 'home board' that takes such decisions. Sometimes, especially in smaller organisations, this responsibility is largely exercised, in effect if not in theory, by one man, corresponding in business terms to 'our founder and chairman' or to a certain type of managing director. In a Christian organisation this is likely to be the man who originally 'had the vision' and who over many years has given time, effort and often such money as he can devote to the work in order to realise what may originally have seemed a visionary dream. He is likely to be a strong personality, hard-working, quick to see possibilities and to seize opportunities. He may well be a successful businessman, possibly somewhat authoritarian ('How else can we get things done?') and with a strong and simple faith in God.

Where a man like this plays a leading part in establishing and guiding a Christian organisation, it is not at all surprising that the result should resemble a 'business' rather than a 'mission' which, by contrast, will tend to be dominated by clergy and to see itself as an institutional arm of the church. In the case of FEBA it is interesting that the Council includes no clergy, and no full-time Christian worker. For some time it had no member with missionary experience. It may be equally significant that there is no woman member; neither the world of business nor the church (as a whole) attaches much apparent value to the contribution of half the human race.

Painful experience has led *missions* to realise the importance of *co-operation*, both among themselves and with churches in the countries where they work. Once upon a time, things were very different, with denominations and inter-denominational missions competing against each other and duplicating activities — all with comparatively little reference to the views of local church leaders. Today, a 'gentleman's agreement' ensures that there is as little overlap as possible, though groups which are out of sympathy with 'establishment' do carry on independent activities in competition with the rest.

Here too the world of Christian broadcasting seems to have less in common with the world of church and mission, than with the competitive world of business. At one level this can be seen in a situation such as existed in Beirut at the time when FEBA accepted responsibility there. At that time, three studios (at least) were providing programmes: ELWA, TWR and Southern Baptist. For various reasons, TWR and ELWA decided to withdraw, and ELWA invited FEBA to take over their studio, but even so two studios remained working independently. (At the time of writing, the work has ceased and the future is uncertain.)

Another manifestation of competition is the way in which each programming agency appears to work in almost anarchic independence of what others are providing. This tendency can be realised most forcibly by listening to the output of a commercial station or of a Christian one which (unlike FEBA) makes no attempt to ensure balanced programming. Fifteen-minute programmes follow each other, each featuring a different personality, each demanding that letters go to a different address, each completely independent of the other, and never more so than when three or four consecutive 'hymn and a thing' programmes from different sources make it clear that the underlying philosophy is that of Judges 21:25, when 'every man did what was right in his own eyes.'

Nor does there appear to be much formal co-operation between the different programme transmitting agencies. True, the conferences which are held from time to time provide an opportunity to exchange information and enable workers from different organisations to meet, but the nature of the medium encourages what might appear to be a rather light-hearted and irresponsible attitude to decisions about reception areas. Various parts of Africa, for example, are already receiving programmes from CORDAC, ELWA, TWR, FEBA and other stations. Yet the situation in Christian radio is such that it would not be at all surprising if another two or three (twenty-two? twenty-three?) Christian men possessing 'vision' and sufficient charisma to raise funds were to establish as many new stations in the Mediterranean and on Atlantic islands so as to beam yet more programmes into Africa — without consulting 'brothers in Christ' who supposedly share a common purpose.

Some Indian believers were very surprised when TWR announced the establishment of a medium-wave transmitter in Sri Lanka. They saw this as a clear case of competition rather than co-operation with FEBA. Whatever the intention may have been, the absence in this case of any outward semblance of joint planning strengthened the fears of some that Christian transmitting agencies may easily come to resemble the mutually competitive organisations which make up the world of business.

Conversations with individual workers in Christian radio (transmission and programme supply) uncovered a good deal of concern about what was seen by them as lack of co-operation. But an approach to the transmitting agencies elicited very reassuring responses: 'There is a great deal of consultation . . . The "patchy" nature of short-wave coverage over the vast areas involved means there is room for even more stations . . . so many languages . . . we welcome every effort . . .' All the same, it is clear that the story of Christian radio so far is not outstandingly one of mutual consultation. That there is no attempt (or very little) to select and allocate audiences. The shareholders of any business enterprise would be entitled to ask some searching questions about the reduplication of costly facilities represented by (to give one example only) the co-existence in the Pacific of installations owned by FEBC, TWR and HCJB. The public relations departments of the radio missions imply that every new installation is necessarily a cause for thanksgiving and show no sign of awareness that another viewpoint is possible. The Christian supporters who foot the bill deserve some public explanation of why this overlapping provision of facilities is necessary.

Nor is the situation always much better when it is a question of *co-operating with local churches*. Failure in this respect takes two forms. One is failure to co-operate in programme supply. RVOG was scrupulous about this, insisting that its programmes originate with churches in the areas to which the programmes were directed. This policy not only makes sense in spiritual terms since it means a genuine 'fellowship in the gospel' between Christians transmitting and Christians supplying programmes, but also commends itself as the most obvious way to ensure that the programmes will be suitable for the intended listeners. Indigenisation is not merely a fashionable slogan. It seems extraordinary to take programmes produced in North America and Britain by and for the 'natives' of those parts (often, in point of fact, for the evangelical sub-culture there) and then project them with all the power of modern radio technology at Muslims in Nigeria, Hindus in Uttar Pradesh, Buddhists in Thailand, and animists in Papua. The radio wavelength may be suitable; the cultural wavelength is almost completely inappropriate.

There are only two exceptions to this condemnation. Some listeners in non-western cultures are in various respects westernised. Thus the existence of stamp collectors all over the world justifies a programme like RWW's 'Hobby of Kings' and some programming in English is appropriate within a culture such as India where English is a second language. (Even in this case there are three further points to consider: (1) Ideally these programmes should be made by Indian believers; (2) Indians prefer BBC English to American English which many find hard to follow; (3) The Church in India will be largely ineffective until it learns to present Christianity — whatever language may be used — in Indian terms).

The second exception is that using western programmes may be excused if no other suitable material is available. FEBA programming, for example, leans rather heavily on British and American sources which will appeal to the westernised Indian church rather than to unbelievers or to Christians who have integrated their faith with Indian culture. But FEBA is increasingly trying to seek out and promote more suitable material from the subcontinent in spite of difficulties caused by the western bias of many Indian evangelicals and the dearth of Christians trained in the art and science of communication. The ultimate aim is to use no English programmes produced outside the reception area but achieving this depends on funds and programme specialists becoming available. FEBA feels it would be irresponsible to act solely as a transmitting agency, and not to do everything possible to improve the quality of the programmes transmitted, in content as well as in technical expertise. Western evangelical and evangelistic programmes, however good a few of them may be, are, in the last resort, no more than a second best.

Failure to work with the indigenous church is seen at the receiver as well as the microphone. Local churches and Christian radio agencies might be expected to co-operate in following up listeners who write to programme producers. We explain elsewhere (pp. 104f) why this is not as simple as it might appear, but it is hard to avoid feeling that some programme suppliers and transmitting agencies are rather complacent about their failure to work with local churches. It must be added that many local churches in reception areas (like many in the UK and USA?) are not able to provide the personal visitation and pastoral care that such co-operation would make necessary. When Jesus gave his disciples the Great Commission of Matthew 28:19, which is referred to several times in these pages, he told them to 'Go!'. In other words, as John Stott points out forcefully (*Christian Mission in the Modern World*, Falcon, London, 1975, pp. 55f.), 'there should be no proclamation without presence.' Something important is missing if the voice of the gospel is a disembodied one, and to engage in Christian broadcasting without the co-operation of the local church in the reception area is at best an unfortunate and unbiblical necessity.

Still at the receiving end — local churches should be able to make use of the programmes, whether by advertising them or providing parallel or supplementary teaching. But there is little sign of this. So far as FEBA is concerned, it is a valid point that advertising the programmes has had to wait until the signal was sufficiently strong to ensure consistently adequate reception. But however plausible the reasons advanced, one is left wondering whether Christian radio may not in fact be the last stronghold of western religious imperialism. Local churches, hospitals, schools, even theological colleges are increasingly taken over by indigenous workers, but for good reason radio is an exception. It costs so much, it demands a degree and kind of technical expertise that is still comparatively rare. Its practitioners tend to function within a cultural and racial ghetto, removed by thousands of miles from the people they seek to reach for Christ. There is clearly a danger — and a very real one in some agencies — of perpetrating divisive attitudes that the church as a whole has abandoned.

It must be admitted that involving local Christians is not always easy. The experience of Far East Broadcasting Associates of India illustrates the difficulties of indigenisation experienced by all sorts of organisations, secular as well as Christian. FEBAI is staffed almost completely by indigenous workers, but two ultimately unsuccessful efforts to find an indigenous leader to direct the team have ended in failure, with much spiritual and emotional distress to all concerned. It seemed like an admission of defeat when Allen Buckwalter took up once more, at the end of 1974, responsibilities he thought he had relinquished for good. At the time of writing, FEBA is still trusting God for guidance in selecting the right indigenous worker to lead an enterprise which still depends in part on gifts from the west.

If businesses are used to competition, rather than co-operation, they are also accustomed to *conceal failure;* indeed, they will go to remarkable lengths to preserve the image of progress, creative innovation, expansion and efficiency. It was an inspired advertising gimmick for one business organisation to claim 'we are only the second biggest, so we try harder' but this approach will scarcely be imitated by other concerns.

Here too, it must be confessed, missionaries and missionary societies — indeed the church as a whole — have (in J. B. Philips's vivid phrase at Romans 12:2) allowed the world to squeeze them into its mould. Roman Catholics have coined the word 'triumphalist' for a Christian image that replaces the 'form of the servant' by that of worldly success, but the phenomenon is not confined to any one branch of Christendom.

Although Christians claim to believe in a Saviour who triumphed through defeat they are reluctant to support (financially or in prayer) 'unsuccessful' Christian workers or agencies. The conscientious missionary or evangelist has to fight very hard to avoid giving a dishonest picture of constant 'blessing' varied only occasionally by the attacks of the 'enemy of souls'. Because of this tendency, fellow workers sometimes find it difficult to recognise the description of a situation in which they too were involved!

So there are powerful pressures on Christian radio agencies to 'sell' themselves to the Christian public whose support they need. FEBA has been criticised for painting too rosy a picture of its achievements and it is not a complete answer to say that other similar organisations lay the colours on even thicker. The fact is that Christians don't want to read or hear about failure, except on Good Friday—and they already know there's a happy ending to *that* story!

This book, at any rate, was undertaken on the clear understanding that it was not going to be a white-wash job. So one or two things about 'success' can be simply stated. First, any radio agency can produce dramatic stories of conversions. After all, if people turn to Christ as a result of picking up a fragment of a gospel from the gutter, they may well be changed through listening to a poorly-delivered, cliché-ridden sermon on the radio. Sensational stories prove nothing—except, perhaps, that God works in unexpected ways.

Second, every organisation run by human beings becomes involved in failure and frustration. It is dishonest to pretend otherwise. The fact that the bitter disagreement between Paul and Barnabas (Acts 15:36–40) ultimately had some good results in no way mitigates their failure on this occasion. God can still use his children's failures, but it is futile to deny their existence.

Third, every attempt to draw up a balance sheet for any Christian work is at best provisional and at worst presumptuous. There is no simple way of measuring success in radio work.

As we have said, stories of individual conversions are easy to come by and while they encourage workers and supporters they cannot supply a rational justification for any organisation. Anecdotes about listeners and quotations from letters while equally interesting, have no statistical value. All Christian radio organisations supply figures showing the number of letters received each month. But it is difficult to attach very great significance to these in the light of casual remarks such as the following, made by an administrator in a large programme supplying agency. 'People', he explained, 'don't write when they have nothing to ask for.' Which makes it clear that the number of letters received may depend as much on the free gifts available (the bribes offered, some would say) as on the 'gracious work of the Holy Spirit' to which the organisations concerned would prefer to ascribe their 'success'. And there are other dishonest ways of presenting correspondence figures — for example quoting as if it were typical the best month of the year (possibly one in which a free gift was on offer).

Adequate audience research may seem a possible way of gauging success, but even if research were accurate, the possibility would remain that God might wish to use a method or an agency that did not seem among the most effective measured by this standard.

In the last resort, Christians should know better than to try and balance accounts before the final audit, as Paul points out in 1 Cor. 4:3–5.

FEBA workers who were consulted while this book was being written were open about their doubts. The situation on Mahé, ideal in many respects, has several serious drawbacks. The transmitter is not a large one, by comparison with others. The results of audience research, while in some respects encouraging, present serious problems which must be worked at. The rapid and continuing expansion of FEBA and its concentration on providing buildings and equipment, has placed a severe strain on workers and supporters. But the very workers who have shared these difficulties (among others) with the writers have never suggested that the existence of such problems calls into doubt either the work of FEBA or their own place within this. Because they believe they are where God wants them to be and doing his work, they are able to live with the stresses and uncertainties. Like many (but by no means all) missionaries today they would welcome a general return to the honesty of the first missionary to Europe who not only described in one of his letters how 'great opportunity has opened for effective work and there is much opposition,' but also was not ashamed to confess that at one time 'we were completely overwhelmed; the burden was more than we could bear; in fact we told ourselves that this was the end' (2 Cor. 1:8 — J. B. Phillips).

It is rather disturbing that Christian radio agencies which would claim to be doing today the same work as Paul did in the first century are so reluctant to follow Paul's example in admitting and even 'glorying in' weakness.

The wise businessman looks well ahead. Planned expansion is one of the secrets of success; stagnation can be as much of a danger as mushroom growth. Missionaries, by contrast, have often been dubious about forward planning; they have tended to feel that 'five-year development plans' and 'target figures' come uncomfortably near to telling God what he ought to do. They have tended to be (in secular terms) opportunists, or (as they might prefer to put it) open to the leading of the Spirit. Naturally they have hoped, prayed and worked for growth, but they have seen this in terms of an organic process as depicted in the parables of Jesus (the seed growing secretly, the yeast, the mustard seed) rather than as a result of rational calculation.

Today this dichotomy is being queried, even at local church level, and it is being argued that the Holy Spirit may work just as well through conscious planning as by ad hoc decisions, or irrational impulses. But for reasons that will already have become clear, the men responsible for building Christian radio have always tended to plan like businessmen. The story of FEBA is no exception to this rule. The annual reports refer to progress on Stage I of one project and Stage IIB of another; they set 'goals' for the coming year and 'evaluate' the degree of success achieved in respect of the previous year's goals.

It seems clear that the work of agencies such as FEBA, ELWA and HCJB could not continue without this sort of realistic planning. Certainly FEBA has grown remarkably quickly; indeed some workers and supporters have suggested that growth has been rather too speedy. 'God's way is to use a few men, and to allow natural growth,' said one Indian supporter, who believed that the troubles experienced by FEBAI might well be providential.

Policy decisions about development are taken by the Council of FEBA (corresponding, as we have seen, to the board of a business undertaking). Some of these decisions are, inevitably, both crucial and controversial. We may instance first of all the system of missionary support units described in Chapter 10. Another example is the decision to press on with the various construction programmes on Mahé, including building the reef aerials and installing the Gates transmitter. These put such an appalling and continuous strain upon the overworked staff that one might well doubt the wisdom of the policy. Yet if this work had been postponed inflation would have increased the cost out of all proportion and might have made completion impossible.

It is possible also to argue (as is hinted in Anne Ediger's report on her audience research) that it made very little sense to devote so much money and effort to providing transmitters, aerials and studios while doing so little (comparatively speaking) to ensure a supply of good programmes. This particular problem seems rather of the chicken and egg (which came first?) variety but it entailed a controversial decision.

It is not at all surprising that FEBA workers should feel strongly about issues such as these. Anybody who has worked within any organisation, religious or secular, will remember discussions, more or less good-humoured, analysing and criticising decisions taken by 'the board' or 'the management'.

One of the problems faced by FEBA (and shared, one suspects, by other similar organisations) is the vast distance separating policy makers from executives in the field. Consultation and discussion are not easy across thousands of miles and this means that it is hard to provide for the sort of participation in decision-making that the business world is increasingly being urged to promote. And whereas a business organisation might not hesitate to fly its executive to a first-class hotel for a conference to explain and discuss new policies (off-setting the cost against profits!) few Christian agencies would dare to tell their supporters that funds had been spent (squandered?) in this way. By and large, Christians have a double standard in this context — what they accept as normal expenditure in their personal and professional life they condemn as gross extravagance when undertaken by Christian workers and organisations.

A business run by missionaries or a mission run by businessmen? There can be no doubt that Christian radio — and, it is now being realised, many kinds of Christian service — has a great deal to gain by utilising the experience of men skilled in management, marketing and production. Jesus regretted that the children of light so often showed themselves less shrewd than the children of this world. On the other hand, it is equally clear that allowing 'business methods' to shape the outlook and activities of a Christian organisation will in the long run render it completely useless except as a money-making concern or a toy for the amusement of those who run it.

However grandiose or efficient FEBA (or any similar agency) may appear to be, the ultimate test must be whether it is serving the kingdom of God. The men and women who have given themselves to this enterprise have done so, in the last resort, because they believe that this is what they have been called to do. It is their way of responding to the challenge Jesus left with his disciples of every generation: Go and make disciples of all nations.

We have already seen why it is impossible to make any

definitive and final assessment of either the methods used in Christian radio or the arguments put forward to justify it. But Matthew 28:19 provides the motivation for the people who are doing the work. It also gives a good deal of guidance to anybody who takes seriously the question raised in this chapter.

CHAPTER 12

A New Kind of Missionary?

OLD IMAGES TAKE a long time to die and a surprising number of people cling to the traditional picture of the missionary. They no longer imagine him in pith helmet and shorts, but still see him, Bible in hand, exhorting, evangelising, expounding, while simple, sinful folk gather round the messenger of the gospel and civilisation.

Of course many missionaries are occupied with evangelism, Bible teaching and pastoral work. But 1977 offers another and rather different missionary image. Here are the trained doctor, nurse and teacher, using their professional skills to heal bodies and feed minds, showing the love of Christ in action and taking time now and again to pass on a simple 'gospel message' or 'word of testimony.' We are all familiar with mission hospitals and mission schools and more recently still have begun to recognise the need for missionary farming centres. Christian caring and helping agencies are a fulfilment of the promise of Jesus that his disciples would do greater works than he (John 14:12).

Neither of these missionary images shows much resemblance to the work of the men and women who form a radio transmitter team. The basic difference does not consist in the new skills required so much as in the fact that the workers have no direct personal contact with the people whom they are serving. Letters provide the only link and few of them receive these. They have no opportunity to respond to the needs of suffering and deprived humanity. Nobody looks to them as examples of

Christian living. They rarely preach sermons or (except by letter) counsel individuals. They do their work as administrators, secretaries, engineers and technicians just as if they had never left their secular calling; and they may find themselves in a Christian ghetto with little opportunity of even 'witnessing' to their colleagues.

It's an unnatural way for Christians to live, especially if they are full-time Christian workers, committed by definition to an all-out effort to extend the Kingdom of God and bring other people to Christ.

Many Christian transmitter teams are situated in places where there is an opportunity to participate in local Christian broadcasting, or engage in direct evangelism, so that the workers are able to devote some of their leisure to such activity, just like other Christians all over the world, who work to earn their living and use their spare time in Christian service. HCJB and ELWA even run mission hospitals.

For the FEBA workers on Mahé, there is less opportunity to do this sort of work. The island's population is small; and although many of the team are involved in Bible class teaching, youth work and house meetings and local church work, the possibilities are limited chiefly because understaffing at the station makes heavy demands on time and strength.

This state of affairs adds considerably to the strain of working on Mahé. Most missionaries find some compensation for the stress of their work in seeing lives changed by the gospel, but satisfaction is to a great extent denied to the team on Mahé.

Yet basically they are missionaries in the most traditional sense, for they have left the security and comfort of their homes so that others may hear the good news about Jesus. Some of the FEBA workers are in fact members of other missionary societies. Jim Hunter and Nishi Sharma, for example, who are studio manager and engineer respectively in Delhi, are seconded from BMMF, as Bob Twynham-Perkins was from ICF (see p. 42), while David and June Henderson belonged to RBMU.

All the same, their skills, training and daily work are very different from those usually associated with missionaries. Producer, studio engineer, office manager, secretary, transmitter engineer, frequency manager — these are not the occupations that most people think of when they meet a missionary. It's not only that they might have been doing just the same work had they never joined FEBA; their opportunities for what most would regard as 'Christian service' are more limited than if they had stayed at home.

It must also be said, however, that they work on very different terms from what they might normally expect. As we have seen, living standards, hours of work, salary and holidays bear no resemblance at all to what would be taken for granted by *unskilled* workers in Europe and N. America. If sacrificial giving is the test of whether a Christian is also a 'missionary' then there can be no doubt how one should classify FEBA staff.

Organisations like FEBA are sometimes described as 'functional missions'. The term is new, but the concept is familiar. A functional mission exists in order to provide some specialist service to benefit the church. Perhaps the Bible societies were the first examples; they did not so much attempt direct evangelism as provide the means whereby others could evangelise. Other well known functional missions are the Wycliffe Bible Translators and the Missionary Aviation Fellowship.

It is inevitable that any functional mission should rely to a great extent upon the technical expertise of its workers; without this resource the mission would be unable to carry out its specialist work.

So what are the qualifications for being a FEBA 'functional missionary'?

1. It is natural to begin with specialist qualifications and experience. Quite obviously, no amount of 'spiritual' development can equip an individual to service transmitting equipment. The official 'job description' comprises 'transmitter operator, maintenance and modification; aerial selection and

frequency management. A high level of technological skill is required.' In the reef aerial maintenance department 'masts and concrete bases have to be protected against the sea. Guy wires need to be checked and adjusted to the correct tension. Automatic switching gear needs servicing.'

One might think there would be a shortage of committed Christians qualified for some of these jobs. But probably there are even fewer able to work efficiently in the Programme Department. The work here includes: 'development of programme philosophy; programme schedule planning; announcing and continuity; production of magazine programmes.' It's true that Christian radio has a tradition of learning these skills 'on the job', but this is scarcely an adequate substitute for experience of the competitive world of secular radio. Around the globe, Christian radio stations are competing in the 'international league' and there is an increasing need for recruits who have gained expertise with the big national radio networks, the sort of people who enjoy the work and whose competence would mark them out for promotion.

In the same way, the general maintenance work required and the clerical and secretarial support, call for competence and enthusiasm. No missionary organisation can afford to accept workers who have consistently failed in their 'secular' employment.

2. Before mentioning the 'spiritual' qualifications which some readers would have expected to see placed first, there is another essential: ability to get on with other people. Some find this easy — for others it is a goal scarcely to be achieved in this life. But there is no room on any mission station, and certainly not on Mahé, for the sort of individualist who cannot work with other people. A Christian radio station is not a one-man band.

Under this heading we may include willingness to work with fellow Christians in spite of disagreeing about doctrine or church order. FEBA has a basis of faith but within this framework there is happily room for a great deal of diversity. The person who 'majors in minors' and expects everybody else to accept his or her personal views on disputed issues can provoke a great deal of stress in a small community — and will probably not be happy there, anyway.

Perhaps it is in this context that we should refer to Bible College training. FEBA often advises young candidates, in particular, to spend a year or two at a Bible College, although this can obviously be no substitute for the essential experience mentioned in (1). But life in a Christian community can certainly aid growth in the qualities listed under (2) and although Christian radio may not seem to demand much academic theological knowledge, programmers in particular will benefit from systematic study of their faith, and most prospective workers recognise the need for strengthening the foundations of their Christian commitment.

3. 'Hold fast to Christ, and for the rest be totally uncommitted,'[1] advised a Christian historian in the aftermath of the Second World War. Personal commitment to Jesus Christ is essential for all missionary work, which makes sense only in the context of whole-hearted determination to tell the whole world the good news about Jesus. Anybody who is not working 'for Christ's sake' is likely to be worn down by the limitations and frustrations of the job.

Commitment to Jesus Christ is also a necessary protection against the corrosive effect of the inevitable question: Is it all worthwhile? It's not only anxious children who are tempted to dig up the soil where they have sown their seeds! For a Christian, the only guarantee against such anxiety and self-interrogation is the assurance of being in the place where he or she is intended to be.

But emphasising this aspect of Christian commitment calls into question the whole traditional view of the missionary vocation. If the essential thing is to be in the right place and committed to Christ, then it is unimportant whether the 'right place' is a slot labelled 'missionary'. The story told in these

1. *Christianity and History*, H. Butterfield (London, 1949), p. 146

pages emphasises this. FEBA was brought into being, not by 'missionaries' but by Christians, some 'retired' and some 'in business' who shared a concern which they attributed to the Spirit of Jesus. A great deal of the support and administration in Britain and Australia has come from 'non-missionaries' similarly motivated. Throughout the development of the work on Mahé there has been a constant supply of 'short-term' workers, such as Don Wickens and Calvin Niebling who have certainly not seen themselves as missionaries but were nevertheless convinced that the right place for them, at a given time, was on Mahé. As for Arthur Tuck, he made a decisive contribution on two occasions while working in different places for different employers, before returning to Mahé as an official FEBA worker during 1971–4.

It is natural that a functional mission, such as FEBA, should pose with especial force this question of whether the idea of a 'missionary' as a separate category is helpful or realistic at this point in the story of the church. In this connection, the final word may be the inscription chosen for a plaque fixed to the wall in the FEBAI headquarters at Bangalore. Appropriately, in view of the Commonwealth ethos of FEBA, it was devised by Wyndham Mathieson's Australian wife, Nan, who felt that the wall of the studio in their home (see p. 33) looked bare and unattractive. When the contents of the studio were shipped to India, the chief reception area of FEBA, the plaque went too. In their original context, the words refer to a king of Israel, but to everybody connected with FEBA they find fulfilment in a greater King and express a commitment which, while it transcends conventional 'missionary' categories, expresses the unchanging missionary dynamic:

There went with him a band of men, whose hearts God had touched
(1 Sam 10:26).

HAMMERSMITH PUBLIC LIBRARIES

English Programmes Guide

effective 5th September 1976

Time in GMT

	SUNDAY		MONDAY	
East Africa	0330	Hymn Time	0330	Cities In the Sand
	0345	Sunday Meditations	0345	Radio Today
	0415	Close Down	0415	Close Down
South Asia	0600	Sunday Meditations	0630	Roundabout
	0630	Making Melody	0700	News
	0700	News	0710	Roundabout (contd.)
	0710	Outlook	0730	Out Into Space
	0800	Hidden Treasures	0745	Books In Focus
	0815	Joy Bells	0800	Radio Today
	0830	Close Down	0830	Close Down
	1535	Radio Newsreel	1535	Radio Newsreel
	1550	Back to God Hour	1550	Gospel Record Shop
	1620	A Visit With Mrs. G	1605	Jesus Calls
	1635	Hymn Time	1620	Back to the Bible
	1650	Close Down	1650	Close Down
NE Africa & W Asia	1730	Hidden Treasures	1730	Gospel Record Shop

	THURSDAY		FRIDAY	
East Africa	0330	Story Time	0330	Searching For Truth
	0345	Radio Today	0345	Radio Today
	0415	Close Down	0415	Close Down
South Asia	0630	Roundabout	0630	Roundabout
	0700	News	0700	News
	0710	Roundabout (contd.)	0710	Roundabout (contd.)
	0730	Personally Speaking	0730	Panorama
	0745	Crime Detection *OR* Music Made Easy	0745	A Visit With Mrs. G
	0800	Radio Today	0800	Radio Today
	0830	Close Down	0830	Close Down
	1535	Radio Newsreel	1535	Radio Newsreel
	1550	Break for Music	1550	Panorama
	1605	Hidden Treasures	1605	Keyboard Melodies
	1620	Back to the Bible	1620	Back to the Bible
	1650	Close Down	1650	Close Down
NE Africa & W Asia	1730	Personally Speaking	1730	A Visit With Mrs. G

TUESDAY

0330	Gospel Record Shop		
0345	Radio Today		
0415	Close Down		
0630	Roundabout		
0700	News		
0710	Roundabout (contd.)		
0730	A Short Guide to Musical Instruments	*OR* 0730	Cities In The Sand
		0745	Com-munication
0800	Radio Today		
0830	Close Down		
1535	Radio Newsreel		
1550	Youth Takes The Air		
1605	Cities In The Sand		
1620	Back to the Bible		
1650	Close Down		
1730	All Kinds of Music		

WEDNESDAY

0330	Out Into Space
0345	Radio Today
0415	Close Down
0630	Roundabout
0700	News
0710	Roundabout (contd.)
0730	The Storyteller
0745	Focus On Physics
0800	Radio Today
0830	Close Down
1535	Radio Newsreel
1550	Personally Speaking
1605	The Wondrous Story
1620	Back to the Bible
1650	Close Down
1730	Out Into Space

SATURDAY

0330	A Visit With Mrs. G
0345	Radio Today
0415	Close Down
0630	Men, Manners and Music
0700	News
0710	Saturday Review
0800	Radio Today
0830	Close Down
1240	DX Postbag (alt. Sa)
1535	Radio Newsreel
1550	Jimmy Hunter 15
1605	All Kinds of Music
1635	Grace Outreach
1650	Close Down
1730	Jimmy Hunter 15

FEBA Seychelles offers varied listening

CHRISTIAN TEACHING

Back to the Bible — Grace Outreach
Hidden Treasures — Jesus Calls
Personally Speaking — Radio Today
Search For Truth — Sunday Meditations
The Wondrous Story

MUSIC

All Kinds of Music — Break for Music
Gospel Record Shop — Hymn Time
Jimmy Hunter 15 — Keyboard Melodies
Making Melody

RADIO MAGAZINES

Outlook — Panorama
Roundabout — Saturday Review
Youth Takes The Air

CHILDREN'S

A Visit With Mrs. G — Joy Bells
Story Time

DRAMA

Crime Detection — The Storyteller

SCIENCE AND EDUCATION

Books In Focus — Cities In The Sand
Communication — Focus On Ph
Men, Manners & Music — Ou

Abbreviations and Addresses

BBC: British Broadcasting Corporation

BMMF: Bible Medical and Missionary Fellowship

CMS: Church Missionary Society

CORDAC: Christian radio station in Burundi, sponsored by Central African Broadcasting Co. Inc.
B.P. 1140, Bujumbura, Burundi
PO Box A, Friendswood, Texas

DX(–er): person who listens to short-wave broadcasts as a hobby

ELWA: Christian radio station in Liberia, sponsored by the Sudan Interior Mission
PO Box 192, ELWA Radio, Monrovia, Liberia
84 Beulah Hill, London SE19 3EP
Ray G. de la Haye, Centerton, Indiana 46116

EMI: Electrical and Musical Industries

FEBA: Far East Broadcasting Association – Christian radio organisation associated with FEBC and operating a station in the Seychelles Islands
Sky Waves, St Paul's Road, Woking
Surrey GU22 7EA

FEBAI: FEBA–India

FEBC: Far East Broadcasting Company – Christian radio organisation
Box 1, Whittier, California

FEBCOM: Telegraphic address of all FEBC Radio International Stations and Studios

HCJB: Christian radio station associated with the World Radio Missionary Fellowship Inc.
63a Main Street, Bingley, W. Yorks BD16 2HZ
Opa Locka, PO Box 691, Miami, Florida 33054

ICF: International Christian Fellowship

QSL: Acknowledgments of Reception reports compiled by listeners

RAP: reef aerial project

RBMU: Regions Beyond Missionary Union

RVOG: Radio Voice of the Gospel – Christian radio station in Ethiopia, sponsored by the Lutheran World Federation Broadcasting Service and closed in 1977 by the Ethiopian Government.

RWW: Radio Worldwide – Christian programme supplier, radio project of the Worldwide Evangelization Crusade (WEC)
13 Harold Road, London SE19 3PU

TWR: Transworld Radio – Christian radio organisation
175 Tower Bridge Road, London SE1 2AS
560 Main Street, Chatham, New Jersey

SAGM: South Africa General Mission (now AEF-Africa Evangelical Fellowship).